YOUR
PROSPEROUS
MIND

YOUR PROSPEROUS MIND

Discover what you really want,
what's holding you back,
and how to get new results

Aaron Anastasi

NEW DREAMERS

Editing by Chelsea Richardson
Cover designed by John Carr & Estée Ochoa
Interior designed by Dotti Albertine

ISBN 978-0-9970351-1-7

Printed in the United States of America

First Edition

CONTENTS

CONTENTS

INTRODUCTION

I don't know about you, but I have a deep sense of inadequacy that underlies many things I do—especially the things that matter most to me. Now, because of the work I do as a coach, I know cognitively that this feeling of insufficiency is simply a racket I'm making up, living in, and choosing to believe. But that doesn't make it seem any less real or debilitating, as I embark on new challenges.

As I write these words, it's 4:33 AM, and I'm in a hotel room in St. Louis, Missouri. I've been awake for the past two hours thinking about being on set, five hours from now, acting in a commercial in which I'm one of two leading characters and will be expected to work with the director to improvise some comedy within the scene.

"Come on, it's just a commercial," you might be thinking. And I don't disagree. It's not *that* big of a deal. It's not a feature film starring Meryl Streep, or directed by Martin Scorsese. So why did I call the concierge at 3 AM and have them send up a packet of Alka-Seltzer and a bottle of water?

I'm not going to give you some storybook ending about how everything worked out and it was great. I don't know how it's going to turn out yet, and that's the point.

Wherever you are in life right now, you don't know how the next endeavor, project, or opportunity is going to work out. Sometimes that can be pretty scary—even terrifying or debilitating.

That's where *Your Prosperous Mind* comes in.

This book will give you the tools necessary to be successful amidst the chaos, insecurity, and uncertainty of everyday life. It will help you access and strengthen your uniquely prosperous mind and allow you to thrive in a fast-paced world, as you pursue the voice that calls you to your most heroic self.

I've said it before: I'm no guru—I'm just a regular dude who has stumbled on some principles and ways of being that have produced tremendous results in my life and the lives of my clients. And in the pages that follow I want to tell you about those things in the hopes that you will also experience unprecedented results in your own life, hopefully more than you could ever ask for or imagine.

I believe that is possible, probable even. Because the small shifts in thinking that are taught in this book can yield huge, real-life results.

What Makes This Book Different?

Unlike many of books in the self-help genre, I'm not trying to *get* you somewhere in order for you to have a more prosperous mind and life; I believe you already have all you need. You are not deficient. My goal here is to facilitate a few small shifts in your thinking that will help you approach your goals from a different place and mindset. Achieving success is less about *doing* something differently, and more about choosing a different way of *being*.

Some of your actions will naturally change as your way of being changes, and so will the level and quality of those actions. But your actions are a symptom of your overall way of being and I'm not interested in focusing on symptoms. It's not efficient enough. I want to go straight to the root cause of breakdown in your life in order to maximize efficiency and impact. And in most cases, the root cause is some kind of disconnect or breakdown within your *way of being*, that is, how you see yourself and the world around you, and what you think is possible.

This book assumes that you already have a prosperous mind, because you do. Now, whether you're currently accessing it to the degree that would be most resourceful to you is a different story. I'm guessing you wouldn't be reading this if you were all maxed out on your potential prosperity (financially, relationally, altruistically, creatively, and otherwise). The primary goal of this book is to give you the keys to unlock the tools within your prosperous mind to achieve new results in your life.

The Catalyst for Writing This Book

I was compelled to write this book because of the distinct memory I have of the pain and shame I felt for so many years, not having the courage or wherewithal to achieve the things I really longed for. I truly believed that my dreams—many of which have now come to fruition— were absolutely impossible for me to attain. I was stuck in a prison where the walls were lined with the lies that I believed, like:

"I'm not good enough."

"Success is for exceptional people, not a regular person like me."

"Making money is hard."

"I don't know the right people."

"I'm too far behind."

"My limited résumé and lack of experience eliminate that possibility."

"My age eliminates that possibility."

"My financial situation eliminates that possibility."

"There's something inherently wrong with me."

And here's the real kick in the butt: those thoughts never completely went away. It's not like they disappeared through some spontaneous enlightenment and then I was able to create a new life. No; instead I learned how to access the tools of my prosperous mind in the midst of this barrage of negative thoughts and emotions. Finally, I began creating the life I wanted, and continued to turn down the volume on those limiting thoughts.

More to the point, I learned how to recognize these voices for what they were instead of taking them at face value. And I want to show you how to do the same.

Within a couple of months of applying the *prosperous mind* principles in this book, I began to see some pretty dramatic results in my relationship with the woman who is now my wife, my satisfaction in life, and my income.

Then, after a couple years of continuing to apply these principles, I was in a fun, adventurous marriage with a woman I call my soulmate; my income quintupled; and I was now finally making an impact in the world with a large social media following of 20 million views and 250,000 followers, a full coaching roster of industry-leading clientele, an Amazon bestselling book, and several profitable businesses and investments.

I hesitate to say these things because they sound pompous or braggadocious, but I want to illustrate that these principles just flat-out work—even for a regular guy like me—and they're much easier to apply than you probably think.

For example, one of my clients transformed a one-million-dollar consulting business into a three-million-dollar business in the time we worked together. Another client went from producing seven-thousand-dollar music videos to producing up to 1.3-million-dollar videos for celebrity artists, and he recently won a VMA Award on top of that. Two of my other clients just got signed with the world's largest and most prestigious agencies in their respective industries.

And I could go on and on.

There is a key, several keys in fact, that will give you access to your prosperous mind and allow you to unlock greater possibility and greater results than you ever have before. I will share with you the practical—and sometimes unusual—step by step key principles and ways of being throughout this book.

The principles, strategies, and steps in this book can be used to achieve extraordinary results; whether you're stuck in life or you're already crushing it and are ready for the next big challenge. This book will show you how to see and take hold of options and opportunities that most people won't and don't.

PART I

GETTING STARTED

1

Can I Become a Great _____?

*"The question isn't who is going to let me.
It's who is going to stop me."*
~Ayn Rand

One of the most frequent questions I get from the people I coach is, "Can I become a great _____?" They're not asking if it's possible; they're asking if it's possible for *them*. There is a fundamental flaw in the context of this question, and it reveals a certain belief system. It's an assumption that the power (the money, the success, the opportunity, etc.) is out *there* somewhere rather than inside of us. It's an unconscious way of seeking permission and approval from others.

It makes sense that this type of thinking would be drilled into our heads, since it was the way the world worked for the first decade or so of our lives. Anything we wanted came from our parents or guardians, the ones who held all the power. If we wanted to get something for ourselves we had to please them; we had to win their approval and get their permission. This system grew to be cemented in our minds. When our parents or guardians gave us accolades—when they approved of us—it was generally because we were well behaved and didn't embarrass them. We pleased the ones who held all the money, power, toys, and bubble gum to get what we wanted from them. They were also the ones who most often gave us our first criticisms, so we learned from them how to avoid being reprimanded for doing the wrong thing or standing out in some way.

That system worked fine when we were kids, but doesn't serve us well as we become adults and seek to achieve our long-term goals. In fact, a life riddled with seeking permission and approval and attempting to avoid ridicule most often leads to poverty, broken relationships, and a half-hearted pursuit of dreams.

Understand that the battle of being a great singer or entrepreneur, or any other dream profession, begins in the mind. It begins with realizing that the power is in you. And this power I'm talking about is not some out-there concept or something without real-world application. The power lies in *choice*.

You have the power to choose. You have the power to give yourself permission to take action. As long as we believe that someone else holds the power, we assume a victim position, remain stuck, and become even more firmly rooted in our complaints, excuses, and destructive worldviews that keep us from stepping up.

The cycle of pleasing others and seeking approval never fulfills itself. Even if we believe we've finally pleased the people in our lives, we wake up the next day and fear that they've forgotten it or that it didn't "take," so we start all over again. It's no way to live; believe me—I know from experience. This is one of the reasons I avoided pursuing a career as an actor and filmmaker for nearly a decade—until I finally gave myself permission.

Give yourself permission; choose to be the arbiter of your own destiny. Don't wait around and hope someone else will choose you." As author Seth Godin says, "No one is going to pick you. Pick yourself." We live in a time where choosing ourselves and creating something of value to offer the world are more possible than ever before. Every day people create something, throw it up on YouTube, and change their lives forever. I know because I'm one of them, and just like you (or maybe *unlike* you) I had no idea what the hell I was doing—still don't!

Are you hesitating to make a choice that would put you on the path toward fulfilling your dream? Give yourself the permission to embark on that path by simply choosing to move in that direction. It doesn't matter who you feel may or may not let you; the real question is who is going to stop you. You see, you are the one who gives the permission. Once you choose to give yourself permission, then a whole world of possibility opens up for you. You are the only one who is preventing yourself from taking action toward being, doing, or having what you want.

2

I Just Don't Know How

"I'm always doing that which I cannot do,
in order that I may learn how to do it."
~Pablo Picasso

One of the biggest obstacles to having success in life is the "how" hurdle or, as I call it, the "how" *lie*. With very little exploration, if any, we determine that we would really like to do something (be a great singer, make more money, start a business, have better relationships, and so on) but just don't know *how*.

The only problem with this line of thinking is that it just isn't true.

With the resources available to us now, there is very little mystery about how to be successful in any area. There are endless books and YouTube videos and seminars that lay out the exact details of how others have gone before us and experienced tremendous success. In fact, the more innovative someone has been in reaching their success, the more detailed they are in laying out their exact strategy, because they are so proud of themselves for having done it.

So, if it's not really about knowing "how," then what actually keeps us stuck?

I remember a few years ago sitting with my coach in Solar de Cahuenga, a coffee shop in Hollywood, California and telling him that I wanted to have a career as an actor but I just didn't know how because I didn't know where to start.

He said, "I don't believe you."

You can imagine my shock and defensiveness. My thought process was somewhere along the lines of, "How do you know? Who are you to say? How dare you?"

But he was absolutely right.

I didn't *really* want to be an actor. My current reality was attesting to the fact that I didn't really want that, because I hadn't taken a single step in that direction for years.

You see, the "how to" lie was equally matched with the "want to" lie. Neither was true. It wasn't true that I wanted to, but simply didn't know how; rather, I knew how but I didn't want to go in that direction.

Now, that's a little extreme, of course. I did want to be an actor, to some degree, right? But my "want to" meter was at about a one or a two and needed to be cranked way up if that dream were ever going to turn into a reality. The answer to the "how to" question is discovered along the way, once that "want to" element is cranked up enough to actually get you into action.

The "want to" factor, or desire to achieve your dream, doesn't have to be dependent on whether you think you have natural talent or have the right connections or know a bunch about the "how to" factor already. Your desire to achieve doesn't have to be based on anything other than desire. And when that desire is cranked up enough, all the "how to" elements become obvious.

When I look back on my life and the few successes that I've had—amidst the tremendous amount of failures—I realize I knew little to nothing about how to achieve the success I wanted before I began to pursue it.

For instance, I remember when I started college. I went to a small school in Tennessee called Lee University. I had a strong desire to excel, since I knew I wanted to go to graduate school afterward, but I felt as though I had a disadvantage because I never really studied in high school and certainly never spent the time and effort to learn good study habits. So, once I got to college, my desire to achieve was high, but I didn't have the slightest understanding of *how* to be a successful student.

I had this friend, also my roommate, who was a rock star when it came to study habits, and, subsequently, getting good grades—the real result I was after. So, I shadowed him and copied everything he did most of my freshman year, which meant a lot of hours studying in the library. He found that while the library wasn't necessarily as fun or inspiring as studying at a coffee shop or in the student center, for example, he could get two or three times as much work done without the distractions. Another valuable tactic was to copy all the due dates for all the papers and projects for each class into a physical day planner, with reminders penciled in one, two, and three weeks prior to the due date. This way I always knew what the priority was for that week and no project came as a surprise. He gave me a series of small, basic tips like those that had a tremendous impact on my studies.

Two years later, at the beginning of my junior year, I was asked by the faculty to teach a class on successful study habits for all the incoming freshmen, since I had maintained a 4.0 GPA throughout my freshman and sophomore years. Then, two years later, I ended up getting into my number one choice of graduate school.

I'm not special. Believe me. I'm no different from you. I had to work twice as hard as everyone else to excel— actually, about three times as hard. On average, I noticed that I spent about three times as many hours studying as my friends and other classmates did in order to get grades comparable to theirs. I'm a very slow reader and often (still) have to reread material several times in order to really understand it. This was particularly true when I went to graduate school. I could read a section of a textbook two or three times and still have no clue what it was talking about.

But I didn't mind once I realized how much the end result mattered to me. The amount of work wasn't a hindrance once the desire to achieve hit a critical enough mass to get me into action and down the path toward success.

So, how do we crank up our desire to achieve?

Think about the kind of life you would like to attain. Consider what benefits you would enjoy if you could materialize this desire into reality. You can make a mental list (or better yet, write it down) of the benefits that you would experience if you had whatever it is that you want. This works best if you can vividly imagine the rewards that would come with achieving your goal.

I had a few different motivations. A major one came from the fact that the university would cover half of my tuition if I kept my GPA at or above a 3.7, and grants and scholarships would cover the rest. This meant I wouldn't have to get a part time job and instead could be a full-time student. The second motivation was getting into a competitive program at a highly respected graduate school.

The list doesn't have to be very long. It just has to include benefits that really set a fire under you and get you into action.

So, back to the coffee shop with my coach. He asked me about the "how to" problem, and what it might take to become an actor. And I knew the answer. I actually had a pretty good handle on what it would take to accomplish this dream. The truth was that I was too scared to pursue it, and I was content to live safely behind my excuses and complaints. I hadn't yet done the work to crank up my level of desire enough to be willing to make sacrifices for the dream, to risk looking foolish, or to commit to a path that was so uncertain.

And, like you, I'm still faced with this decision often. While my response varies at any given time, the thing that remains consistent is that when I actually do choose to crank up the "want-to" factor and get into action toward my end goal, I get far superior results than when I choose safety.

In what area of your life are you telling yourself the "how to" lie? Are you telling yourself that you don't know how to sing? Among the myriad of other resources out there, I've created more content with all my online courses and mini-courses than you could probably even get through in a year's time. Is it that you don't know how to write? The best primer I know is a book by Anne Lamott called *Bird By Bird*. Regardless of what you're telling yourself you don't know how to do, today is the day. Today can be the day that you look back on and say, "Yeah, that's the day it all began." You have what it takes to find all the resources you need to succeed. Believe in your bigness, your strength, and your ability to accomplish great things, because I promise you, there is much more inside of you than you are able to see through your own eyes. The time has come to decide that *the time has come.*

3

I Need More Information First

*"The biggest risk is not taking any risk...
In a world that's changing really quickly,
the only strategy that is guaranteed
to fail is not taking risks."*
~Mark Zuckerberg

One common stuck place for many of my clients (and
certainly still for myself at times) is feeling that they need
more information before they can move forward in an area
that is going to take a certain level of risk. This thought is
closely connected to the "I don't have what it takes" and
"I don't know how" lies, but in this case we hide behind
the never-enough volume of information and console ourselves with the thought that we are being prudent or wise
by waiting. This is also generally connected to a fear that
our pursuits won't be successful, which causes us to not
take risks.

There is, of course, some truth to this idea of needing a certain level of information at certain stages of pursuing a project. Doing your "due diligence" can be very resourceful. Then, once you have done some initial research, the next steps are to make a decision, act, and take a risk.

But instead, we often find ourselves choosing fear. Instead of admitting that fear of failure is holding us back, we get stuck in the purgatory of indecision by telling ourselves we're being cautiously wise. Instead of taking action, we say, "I just need more information before I can move forward."

The non-resourceful part of this—aside from being stuck, uninspired, and uninspiring—is that opportunities pass as we wait, because most opportunities have a shelf life. When we hesitate and deliberate and live in the land of indecision, we often miss the gifts the world has to offer.

I had a missed opportunity recently because of this very problem.

I've had casting directors and other film industry professionals tell me for some time now that my "look" would be a good fit for the show *Nashville,* and the fact that I'm a professional guitar player and singer makes me an even better candidate. So, for the past three to four months, I've been saying to my other acting friends that I really *need* to get in contact with the casting director of the show. And it may even be a good idea to get a Southeast acting agent to represent me and start submitting me as a local hire in that region, since so many films and television shows like *Nashville* are being cast and shot there.

I knew that it would potentially open up opportunities for me if I at least made contact with and sent my headshot to the *Nashville* casting director, but I was stuck in indecision because I needed more information first…or that's what I was telling myself, at least.

I told myself I didn't know *how* to get his contact info (which wasn't true, because I have IMDB Pro and could access that info in under a minute), and I wanted to find out if it would be off-putting to contact him out of the blue, but I wasn't sure who to ask about that.

These are the vague conversations and limiting voices in my head that were keeping me stuck. In my mind I thought I was being wise by waiting to see what the proper route would be, which, of course, was not the case, since I wasn't doing anything to acquire the information needed to move forward. I was just using that as an excuse to stay safe and avoid risk.

If I were more honest with myself, I would have really checked in and realized that I was terrified that I would reach out and be "rejected," that casting would say I'm not actually a good fit or laugh at my "thin" résumé. I preferred continuing to live in the *idea* that I was a good fit for the show and I liked talking about it, so I didn't want to shatter that bragging point by potentially discovering otherwise.

The incident that finally shook me out of my fantasy was an actor friend of mine being booked for a co-star role on *Nashville*. Once I heard about that, I finally jumped onto IMDB Pro, found the email address for the casting director, sent a note of congratulations to my friend, and asked her to confirm that this was the right casting person to contact. She confirmed it and also gave me the contact info for her Southeast acting agent.

I contacted the casting director and the agent that day, sending them my headshot, acting reel (video footage of my on-camera acting) links, and résumé, and heard back from both within 24 hours. While both expressed excitement in staying in contact, both let me know that the episode my friend had booked was the final episode for the season. This meant that there wouldn't be any more opportunities to be booked on the show for several months, that is, *if* the show even gets picked up for another season. Although that opportunity was lost, I actually signed with that agency to represent me specifically for shows being filmed in the Southeast, and within a week they got me an audition for a new Ridley Scott television show.

Given the interest I garnered when I finally did submit my materials to the casting director and agent, I realized that I could have been on their radar for nearly the entire last season of the show. But instead I was caught in the land of waiting for more information. There is no telling how many potential opportunities passed because I didn't spend those fifteen minutes looking up contact information and reaching out months earlier.

Opportunities pass.

Of course this isn't license to go out and make rash, foolish decisions in the name of progress and risk (which I'm not altogether against, as an alternative to being stuck in indecision), but it can be useful to ask ourselves, "Am I stalling because I'm afraid, or is there really a piece of information I still need? If the latter is true, then what exactly do I need before I jump in, and how can I get that information right now? Who can I call *right now*? Or what Google search could I do *right now*?"

The pieces of information we're waiting for before making a decision will not appear until we actually take the risk and make the decision. The desire for more information—and the indecision and stuck place that it can create—is often the very thing keeping us from attaining that information.

There is a great scene in the film *Indiana Jones and the Last Crusade*, where Harrison Ford's character, Indiana Jones, needs to cross a huge chasm, maybe two hundred yards or so across, in order to complete his mission and also save his father, played by Sean Connery. The drop between the two rock structures is a deep, seemingly never-ending abyss. Indiana looks back down at his map and reads aloud, "Only in the leap from the lion's head will he prove his worth." He takes another look at the bottomless pit and the distance to the other side and says to himself, "Impossible. Nobody can jump this." The drama cranks up as we cut to his dad, who is in pain and struggles to say, "You must believe, boy. You must believe." Now the shot goes back to Indiana who says under his breath, "It's a leap of faith." He then takes a deep breath, lifts up his foot, and takes a step off the cliff. But instead of falling to his death, his foot hits solid ground where there appeared to be nothing. As the camera pans around, we see that the small rock path was there all the time but was perfectly camouflaged, blending into the rock pattern on the other side of the chasm.

Risk is a major part of any endeavor in which we want to be successful. Safety is the enemy of progress, yet we tend to fight for safety and comfort as if they were the highest goods. Comfort and safety can be self-sabotaging, as they are in direct opposition to the exciting and adventurous life that is otherwise possible.

Author Ray Bradbury once said, "Living at risk is jumping off the cliff and building your wings on the way down." The information, or the "how," comes after the leap, not before. By avoiding risk, we eliminate the possibility of reaching the maximum amount of joy and passion that we aspire to.

Where in your life is there hesitation right now? What might you be avoiding? What information are you waiting to have before jumping into the deep end? Because the biggest risk you can take in life is not taking any risks at all.

Take a minute to write down one thing you might be avoiding. Do you really need any more information before jumping into the deep end?

PART II

BEING
vs.
DOING

4

Who Am I?

*"Realizing that our actions, feelings and behaviors
are the result of our own images and beliefs
gives us the level that psychology has always needed
for changing personality."*
~MAXWELL MALTZ

Many of my clients believe that they are fixed entities;
in other words, that they are locked into a certain way of
being. They'll say things like, "I'm shy. That's just the way
I am, so I can't really sing in front of people," or they'll say,
"I'm super disorganized. I'd like to be more focused, but
that's just not my personality." They say this as if personality were an unalterable reality—as if they were telling me
how tall they are or what color eyes they have.

I'm actually a big fan of personality tests like Myers-
Briggs® and StrengthsFinder®. I use both in my coaching.
It's a great way to discover the patterns of behavior that
we've created for ourselves and the pros and cons of those

patterns. But notice that I said *created* for ourselves. It's all a creation. We are creative beings who have the power to create the behaviors that are going to serve us most.

The personalities we have created for ourselves and fought to maintain were forged in childhood as a survival mechanism. Our personalities come from patterns of actions and thoughts that helped us get recognition and attention and maintain a sense of safety as a child. Then we take these into adulthood, thinking we still need safety for survival, and this leads us to avoid risk and confrontation and any sort of failure—all of which we associate with self-annihilation.

So we continue to be on high alert for any danger, long after any dangers of childhood have vanished, and exaggerate any perceived danger in order to stay alive. This way of being is in direct opposition to the way of being we need to attain our goals and dreams, which are forged through risk and failure. And while we may not be aware of it, this drive for safety is often still conceptually operative in our lives, guiding our thoughts and behaviors.

Invent a more resourceful personality, a narrative about yourself and the world around you that discounts the stories you made up during childhood, which were based on fear and a limited understanding of how the world works.

So, are we inclined toward certain personality types and thoughts and behaviors? Absolutely. These are the patterns we've chosen and/or allowed to take root passively along the way. In fact, experts of Enneagram or StrengthsFinder will tell you that *all* personality types exist in everyone. We've just carved out a path over time that now occurs to us as a fixed personality type, which is why we fit well into these categories—like introvert and extrovert or being a thinker more than a feeler. These carved out personality types can be extremely helpful to us, allowing us to maximize our proclivities or turn them into success.

The challenge arises when we begin to use our personalities as a way to limit and victimize ourselves, as if we don't have the power to be whatever we are willing to commit to being. When we choose to believe we are powerless in this arena, we limit our perceived possibilities, and forego countless opportunities as a result.

Fortunately, this idea of having a permanent, set-in-stone personality isn't our only option because we are constantly renewing ourselves. We can choose to renew ourselves with new behavior patterns or continue to follow old behavior patterns. Most choose the latter, which is why it appears that people don't have the power to change. The truth is that in any given moment, who you are is up to you—and who you are can change.

Let's take a simple behavior pattern; for example, disorganization. Let's say you believed you're disorganized, and I asked you in what areas you were the most disorganized. You said your desk, the files and documents in your computer, and your car are your most disorganized areas. Then I told you that I was going to pop in unannounced several times over the course of the next month or two, and if you were able to keep everything immaculately organized, then I would give you five million dollars cash, tax free. Do you think you would leave any of those things disorganized for even a second during that time? Of course not. Your desk, car, and computer files would be impeccably organized at all times.

But how is that possible? Disorganization is in your DNA, right? It's a personality type that has been passed down for generations, isn't it?

No. Not true.

When you and I are disorganized, it's because we want to be. We may not think that we want to be disorganized, but the physical universe, our current reality, has proven to us that we prefer disorganization over organization. There's no shame in that; it's merely feedback on what we prefer right now. We can choose a different preference at any given moment.

We've seen a scenario in which we can become extremely and consistently organized for a couple months and, after a while, feel like it's our natural way of being. But right now our desire isn't strong enough to do what it takes to be organized.

Now this is a simple example, but it makes a larger point that has a potentially enormous application. We have the power to become who we need to be in order to get the results that we want in life. And the assumption that we're fixed in thinking or one way of being and powerless in who we are is a victim mindset that keeps us stuck, feeling as though there is nothing we can do to change things.

But that's a lie; we are neither fixed nor powerless.

The shift into a new way of being is a matter of desire, commitment, incentive, and choice. It's not a simple matter of ability.

Who would you need to be in order to take the next step toward your dream? Maybe it would benefit you to be the kind of person who doesn't mind making requests of people who can help. Maybe it would help to be the kind of person who chooses not to be discouraged by disappointments.

Develop the habits you want through practice, and eventually they will become part of "who you are." As Aristotle says, "We are what we repeatedly do. Excellence, then, is not an act, but a habit."

Choose who you want to be—it's all a creation anyway. So choose the "you" who will attain the results you want. Let the actions you take form the personality that will be resourceful to you. Before long, people will see this new behavior as part of your natural personality, because that's what it will look like from the outside.

Let your actions delineate and define who you are, because your identity is within your control.

5

Mind-Shift

*"Problems cannot be solved
by the same level of thinking that created them."*
~ALBERT EINSTEIN

It was a major breakthrough for me when I realized that there are several different ways to look at the same thing. How I choose to see something radically affects my mood, my level of fear, and my motivation to move toward goals that are important to me, whether they're about singing, writing, acting, or creating wealth through my businesses.

For most of my life I've woken up with debilitating fear immediately flooding my mind and attempting to shut me down, first thing in the morning. When I give into those fears—those thoughts, really—and that feeling of being overwhelmed, it fosters a certain perspective that has the ability to affect the first several hours of my day. If left unchecked, additional unwanted thoughts have an easier time creeping in, such as judgments of myself and others, suspicion, fears about money, and ultimately despair.

If I let these thoughts sink into my psyche, they have a way of shaping my entire day. And if each day looks like this, then each week, each month, and eventually my entire life could be determined by those thoughts—unless I choose to intervene.

This negative future is possible for me. And the crazy thing is that it comes down to my perspective, how things are occurring to me, and how I am occurring to myself.

Language is what causes things to occur to us in a certain way, and that occurrence (how life appears to be in any given moment) radically affects our actions and, therefore, the results that we get in life.

"Language" refers not only to the words we use but also the conversation that we are having with ourselves in our heads. Notice as you read these words, which is a form of conversation, that you have another conversation going on in your head about the content you're reading; whether you agree with it, how it may apply to a specific situation that's going on in your life, how you're going to maybe grab a bite to eat after this chapter, and so on.

And this is going on whenever you're in conversation with another person. You know how it goes. When you're talking with someone—let's say someone you just met—you're also having another conversation in your head about the conversation. You could be talking about a comedy show you're about to see, but you may also be having a conversation in your head saying, "Did I really just say that? That was stupid. She probably thinks I'm an idiot. She's really cute. I wonder if my breath stinks. Darn it, I think I forgot to lock my car. Whoa! She just touched my arm. I think she's into me!"

So we're having a conversation about the conversation, and then there is yet another level of conversation going on all at the same time (confusing, right?). That particular type of conversation and thoughts repeat themselves over and over. They have been playing in our minds for so long that we don't even realize that they're there. These latent ideas falsely occur to us as truth and reality.

For example, some of my limiting thoughts tend to be, "You're stupid," or, "You're way behind and too old to pursue this now." Another might be, "You're never going to gain any sort of mastery over this. Just give up." And then some of my favorites (they must be favorites since I choose to entertain them over and over again) are, "No one cares about me," and, "There's something wrong with me," and, "I always fail."

These thoughts aren't necessarily that clear-cut in my mind, unless I really explore them. They mostly occur to me as fear or despair or just an overarching feeling that life is hard. But they come from a very specific thought that I'm rehearsing and choosing to believe.

These limiting voices (stories about how I'm powerless and doomed to despair) repeat in my mind so much that they distort my perception of reality. And if I don't recognize these limiting thoughts for what they are, they have the ability to shape my feelings, my actions, and ultimately my entire life.

The good news is that you and I are not victims of these thoughts. There is a way to proactively cause my life to occur to me differently. And if my life is occurring to me differently, the trajectory of my thoughts could shift, which alters the quality and focus of my actions, and new results become a greater possibility.

Recognizing these limiting voices and exploring *why* we choose to believe them is a very effective way to weaken their leverage in our lives. This is a practice that I'll explore more fully in a later chapter.

Another powerful tool is understanding that future-based language (commitments, declarations, stated goals, and visions) transforms how we occur to ourselves (what we think about ourselves) or how a situation occurs to us (what we think is possible in our lives).

So, if my performance and actions depend on how things occur to me, this future-based language is really something to take note of. This means that if we can get a handle on this future-based language thing, we can motivate ourselves to accomplish just about anything.

Let's use a simple example to illustrate the point. This particular example will connect better with the more introverted readers. Let's say you walk into a room full of people who are all more established than you are in an industry, and you feel intimidated. So, without even realizing it, you encounter a flood of thoughts, maybe something like, "I don't belong here. Everyone knows I'm no good at this. Nobody wants to talk to me. Everybody's judging me. If I just stay quiet, nobody will find out that I don't know what I'm talking about."

Think about how you would see yourself in this moment. Think about your state of *being*. Think about the sense of smallness and powerlessness you might feel. In this state of mind, your actions are going to reflect all of this internal chaos, and you're going to get certain results because of it.

The people in the room would likely be put off by your shy demeanor or maybe think that you're stuck up or boring or awkward, so they might either ignore you or maybe even begin to judge you more harshly. So, we begin to create the very reaction we were afraid of, having no idea it was of our own doing…or undoing, really.

The beautiful thing about this is that we can create a different future, if we have a precise commitment. Let's look at an example of how that might look by applying this strategy.

Let's say before you walked into that room you decided that you were committed to present yourself in a certain way. You were committed to make every person you came in contact with feel accepted, loved, inspired, and encouraged. You decided not to be concerned with how you might look, and instead you were committed to serving others; you shifted your focus to the end user, so to speak. How differently might things look? How differently would you act? The situation hasn't changed a bit, but as you approach it differently you get a different result, because your actions are intimately connected to how you see yourself and your circumstances in any given moment.

In the above example, the first way of approaching a room full of people tends to be automatic. We don't even necessarily realize we're having these kinds of thoughts; it just happens. This automatic way of thinking is a path that leads to our default future (the future that will develop from our established patterns as they are now). The other option is to live into a *created* future, one that we cultivate intentionally.

It's all made up and created anyway, so we might as well develop the way of being that serves us the most. The automatic response, which includes limiting voices about how you don't measure up and how people are judging you, is made up, too. None of those thoughts are necessarily true, but they made it *seem* true in our minds. It felt like reality, but it was simply a made up point of view. But what *feels* like reality becomes the reality we create for ourselves. And since we act based on our perceptions, our results are largely based on our *perceived* reality.

This principle can be applied to nearly any area of your life, large or small. And a series of small shifts can literally change your entire life.

We live into the future that we see coming to us, which is why we must create a clearly stated vision and commitment and live into that, rather than living into the negative thoughts that tend to plague the mind if it's left alone.

That brings us full circle to my own morning of fearful thoughts and the possible default future that I spoke about at the beginning of this chapter. It took me many years to realize that these thoughts were ruining me. I simply thought that I was depressed or sad or unmotivated. The truth was that I was passively living out my default future created by default feelings of inadequacy and despair. Once I figured that out, I got busy making some commitments—ones that I have stuck with and helped me for many years. One thing I do that continues to have a profoundly positive impact on my life is confronting all these thoughts first thing in the morning.

I committed to a practice of spending time in the mornings intentionally filling my mind with the thoughts that I know to be the most resourceful for me. I read quotes and passages that inspire and encourage me. I read through my "I'm Thankful For" list. I sit silently for a while and meditate. I forgive myself for anything I may have done the day before that I feel badly about. I may even say aloud the words, "Thank you," or, "I'm excited for what might be possible today."

If there are a couple of particularly pervasive thoughts that seem to be crushing me, I'll employ another tactic.

I'll write the thoughts down and interrogate them. Like a detective in the interrogation room with a sketchy suspect, I'll question the limiting voice to see if it's really true. I'll meditate on it for little while and see if I can really know for sure whether this thought is realistic or simply a distorted sense of reality. Once I do that I'll then ask myself who I'd be if I didn't believe that thought—how differently would I feel or behave without that thought or belief? When I realize that without the thought I'd feel free, I'm reminded that it's the belief that's making me feel depressed or hopeless, not my circumstances. Then I'll find concrete evidence that contradicts the limiting voice. This radical inquiry has a way of diminishing the limiting thoughts and sometimes even eradicating them completely.

As truth-seekers, we understand that the more we question our limiting voices and confining beliefs, the more we can live in the truth and not in a twisted version of reality. The more we live in truth, the more power we have to serve others and get the things that we want in life.

We get that we have the power to change our level of thinking in order to solve the problems that, often times, we've created for ourselves by giving our default, fearful thoughts more credibility than is necessary.

What are some declarations that you can make for yourself? What are some things that you can be committed to in the next meeting, conversation, or situation that you walk into? This kind of conscious, intentional living is one of the major shifts of mind that begin to radically alter our perceptions of ourselves, how we respond to our circumstances, and, in turn, the results that we get in life.

6

Everything's Going to S#*!

"Tell your heart that the fear of suffering
is worse than the suffering itself.
And no heart has ever suffered
when it goes in search of its dream."
~Paulo Coelho

One dangerous result of worrying is downward spiral thinking. I say "dangerous" because it results in a stuck place—a way of thinking and speaking that diminishes our power to reach our deepest desires and stated visions for our lives.

Downward spiral thinking is present when we find ourselves believing things are going from bad to worse. We speak of walls and roadblocks and gatekeepers, focusing on all that it will take to reach a goal and the probability that it's not possible at all.

All industries and relationships have their own versions of downward spiral talk, about how ten or twenty or fifty years ago this particular endeavor may have been possible, but now with how things have changed, it's a one in a billion chance.

One example of this limiting downward spiral talk comes from a classically trained opera singer I know. The downward spiral goes something like this: "The old ladies who support classical music are all dying and culture is so commercialized now that young people have no interest in opera, so audiences shrink more and more every year." This kind of talk is a resigned way of thinking that excludes possibility and focuses on the difficulty and seeming impossibility of reaching our dreams. It is born out of a scarce way of thinking, according to which the sky is falling and imminent doom is inevitable. The truth is that diminishing audiences only exist in the minds of those who believe the limiting voices, rather than reality.

Downward spiral thinking creates stories about the barriers to what is possible. But these stories only represent one side. It's not necessarily a true story, but as long as we believe it, we function under the assumption that it's true and get the results that that worldview produces—as we talked about in the previous chapter.

Another example is one I heard from an actor friend of mine who has had a decent measure of success, especially with commercials, but was in a slow period of his career at the time. He said to me, "It's getting really tough out there, since movie stars are now doing television, and television stars are now doing commercials. There's no room for actors unless they're already established stars." This kind of thinking is very prevalent among my acting friends.

Interestingly enough—and contrary to his downward spiral thinking at the time—this particular friend is currently in New York filming season two as the lead on a television show on a major network.

When we choose to simply describe situations as we see them—or more appropriately, how they are occurring to us in the moment—we resign ourselves to descriptive language. But descriptive language can only describe; it cannot produce anything new. It's a way of believing that the only possible future is a continuation of what is occurring to us as reality in the moment.

For instance, I might think, "Oh no, I lost another client, and clients are becoming harder and harder to acquire, so I'll probably lose all my clients and go bankrupt," or a repackaged, bandaged-up version of the past, such as, "My last two relationships didn't work out, so my next one probably won't either, especially since people are only becoming more and more shallow and entitled nowadays."

When we let our imaginations runaway, picture worst-case scenarios, and create trends out of a scarce way of thinking, we get stuck, and we stay stuck until we interrupt those thoughts and choose a new way of being and a new story to live into. Instead of adhering to the downward spiral way of thinking when it comes to relationships, you might create a new story and a new commitment, such as, "I'm sure there are a dozen potential partners in my general area. How differently might I behave if I believed that were true?" How could I add more consciousness to the different areas of my life to make them more in line with the types of attributes I'm looking for in a mate?"

A new story and commitment for the client scenario might be something like, "Well, 13th-century Persian poet, Rumi says, 'What you seek is seeking you,' and that may actually be true. I know I've had a powerful impact on my clients' lives up until now, so I'm committed to reaching out to five new people this week who I can serve powerfully, and if a client comes as a result, great, but I will focus on the service and trust that it will come back to me somehow."

One question to ask ourselves in order to get centered on current reality is, "Am I speaking from the mindset of downward spiral thinking or from a mindset of possibility?" Another one is, "Am I seeing the world through an admittedly skewed version of the way things are, given my negative outlook at the moment, or am I choosing to look for opportunities on the path toward success?"

The way we define our realities sets the framework for how our lives and circumstances will unfold. So, if we define reality with downward spiral thinking and allow ourselves to say things like, "Everything's going to s#*!" then our results will reflect that.

Is there an area in your life now where you notice downward spiral thinking, or a resolved, stubborn perspective? Are you willing to question your assumptions about what you "just know" is true? Are you willing to really ask yourself what's good about the situation and what undiscovered opportunities exist that you have been too scared to take advantage of?

The sooner we can recognize—and shift away from—downward spiral ways of thinking, the quicker we can get back onto the path toward our desired goals.

PART III

RACKETEERING

7

My Life Isn't Working

"I am not what has happened to me.
I am what I choose to become."
~Carl Jung

Some years ago I went to a seminar called "Breakthrough" where one of the exercises we did was called "Victim/ Responsible." I sat in a chair facing another participant who sat in a chair directly across from me. The objective was to take one minute to tell a true story about myself in which I was hurt or disappointed or was in some way a victim.

Here's a truncated version of the story I told:

"I've got a terrible migraine right now. I've suffered from migraines since I was a kid. But it's gotten much more severe and frequent over the years. I've seen every kind of doctor you can imagine: neurologists, acupuncturists, chiropractors, allergists, naturopaths, etc.

*So, I've just kind of learned to deal with it and manage
the pain the best I can."*

After I finished telling that story I was asked to tell
the exact same story but this time as if I was completely
victimized, as though I was one hundred percent a victim
of the circumstance. The first time wasn't too far off from
that, but I could certainly crank up the pity party, so I told
it in even more of a sob story fashion:

> *"I've been plagued with migraines since birth, and
> they only get more severe and frequent as time goes on.
> I'm at the verge of despair at all times. There's noth-
> ing I can do about this disease and the tyranny of this
> non-stop pain. I've got no options left. No doctor could
> help, so I was left alone and relegated to hopelessness
> and fear. I'm completely powerless over this debilitat-
> ing affliction that will never get better but will likely
> get worse. Why does this kind of thing always happen
> to me?"*

During this re-telling of the story, I noticed how easy
and second nature it was for me to play into this victim
story and use flowery, descriptive language to manipulate
the listener into buying my "poor-me" narrative.

Finally, I was asked to tell the same story one more
time but this time as if I was one hundred percent responsible for the situation and how it unfolded.

"I've got a migraine right now, but, if I'm honest, it's on me; it's my own doing. I've been getting migraines for long enough to know that sugar, lack of sleep, and alcohol are potential triggers, and together they are a perfect storm. I ignored this reality yesterday, so sure enough, I got a migraine that could have been avoided. I've actually been seeing a new naturopath, and through some changes in my diet, a steady regimen of homeopathic supplements and an air filter in my home, I've recently seen some significant improvements in both the frequency and severity of my migraines."

This exercise had a profound impact on me. I noticed that when I told the story the first time I felt a little disconnected, since I had told the story several times before. And I noticed that telling the story again sapped my energy.

When I told the story from the victim perspective, with victim language like, "There's nothing I can do," and, "I've got no options left," and, "It will never get better," and, "I always get them," I felt drained and powerless. There was a certain destructive comfort in the self-righteousness and self-pity that I enjoyed to some extent. It's almost like the smoker who takes a drag of a cigarette and feels a sense of comfort and relaxation in the moment but is ultimately doing far more harm to the body in the long-term. When using victim language I feel emotionally shut down, unmotivated, and helpless.

An unexpected thing happened when I told the responsible version of the story, the version in which I took complete ownership of how things had transpired. Instead of feeling the weight of hopelessness and resolve, I actually felt empowered. I felt the power of *choice*. I could see in a fresh way how I contributed to what happened. I no longer felt like a victim of the situation but rather a participant in it.

I not only realized that a past situation could look a lot different than it had previously occurred to me, but more importantly that the way I chose to use my words and language radically affected my energy level, enthusiasm, and motivation.

In his book, *Reinventing Yourself*, Steve Chandler talks about this distinction. He calls it "Owner/Victim" and talks about how the quality of life and performance of the Owner is starkly different in terms of relationships, wealth, accomplishments, and disposition. And this all comes from the words that we use, which reveal the thoughts that we think and choose to believe.

Victim language both causes the victim mindset and clearly indicates when one is in the victim mindset. You can always know who you're *being*, or who you're choosing to be, in any given moment by listening to your language.

The trouble with using victim language is that it produces a bad mood, low levels of creativity, a lack of vitality, low energy, and very little imagination. And in this state it is nearly impossible to create good relationships, wealth, or the fruition of our dreams. How could we achieve those things, if all of our faculties for creating the lives we want are shut down? We don't create new things in a victim mindset. We spend our time surviving and reacting instead of producing something of benefit to ourselves and others.

So let's take a look at a couple of examples on both sides of this distinction between Owners and Victims.

Let's start with mine from above: "Why does that always happen to me?" I lived inside of this complaint for many, many years when confronted with a problem or challenge (sometimes I still do). I imagined that the world had it out for me, that I was cursed or that something was wrong with me. I thought that there was nothing that I could do about it, that it was written into my DNA or in the stars or whatever. Either way, I was a victim, and the best I could do was to just ride it out and get used to it. After all, I was powerless to change it.

Not true.

We all have the power to change things; it's in the language that we use and the thoughts we choose to rehearse and believe.

Owners say things like, "How can I use this?" or, "What would I like to create in light of this?" or, "What opportunity exists as a result of this situation?" These questions immediately put the ball back into our court as a force of change. Now the power to create something new is no longer *out there* pressing within but *in us*. Another common form of victim language is saying, "I have to," or, "I have/had no choice." These statements are most common when referring to work, when someone says, "I have to go to work." Deep down, we know that we don't have to go to work. Certainly we don't *have* to go to the particular job that we have at the moment. There are infinitely more options if this job isn't what we really want to be doing. We may not see the other opportunities, but that's generally because we haven't gotten to the point of action. We stay stuck in the thought of "have-to."

The ugly cousin of have-to is got-to, which is often just another way of stating the societal favorite, "I should." This thought assumes there is some kind of parental figure or judge and jury in our minds keeping tabs on our behavior, like somehow we're never quite hitting the mark. "I didn't go to the gym today, but I really *should*. I don't really ever read books, but I know I *should*. I don't drink much water or eat greens but…" We "should" ourselves into a low mood, low energy, and, worst of all, shame.

But there are other options that put us back into the driver's seats of our lives, so that we no longer feel victimized by the perceived judge and jury. "I want to—" or "I'm going to—" or "I'm committed to doing my vocal exercises for five minutes per day, on Mondays, Wednesdays, and Fridays."

Part of the reason we tend to shame ourselves and "should" all over ourselves is because many of us believe that we need to shame or scare ourselves into action. But this is a very low form of motivation. If it works, and I would argue that it generally does not, then it's usually short lived and the task is done without a sense of freedom, imagination, and play—the very things that lead to creative work, effective service, and ultimately wealth.

The victim doesn't realize that this is a chosen narrative. He believes that this victim language is simply the truth about life. The truth is that most often it's not a circumstance or a person that is holding us back from realizing our potential. It's our language. It's the words we use that reveal the thoughts and beliefs that kill our moods, motivation, and energy.

This is important because success comes from staying on the path toward our goals. But it's nearly impossible to stay on that path when our language is constantly derailing us.

The overarching complaint of the victim is, "My life isn't working." If you feel this way about your life or your artistic pursuits, I would encourage you to begin to deliberately listen to the words that come out of your mouth and see whether you are more often in the mindset of the Victim or the Owner.

8

I Can't Get Beyond This Ceiling

"There are no limitations to the mind
except those we acknowledge."
~NAPOLEON HILL

Our underlying contexts and motivations can cause us to continue repeating the same patterns over and over again or to hit a ceiling on how far we will allow ourselves to go. Setting limits on our own progress shows up as a cyclical pattern of failing to achieve in life, by way of unconsciously self-sabotaging.

I say "unconsciously" partially because I don't believe that we destroy our lives consciously. Nearly all living organisms, humans included, are hard-wired for self-preservation. When we engage in self-destructive patterns it's because we're getting something out of them that we believe to be somehow better (and often safer) than an alternative decision. We're not always right, of course, which is why one of the twelve step rehabilitation program slogans is, "My best thinking got me here," that is, at rock bottom and enslaved to a substance or process.

The second reason I use the word "unconsciously" is because the path out of these self-destructive, cyclical patterns that limit our successes in any endeavor is adding consciousness—a greater awareness—to the *why* behind the behavior. Self-destructive behavior is a form of a racket, and the best way to beat a racket isn't to try to rid ourselves of it (another racket) but to be aware of the hidden motivations behind the harmful behavior with it. This way we can make more authentic decisions with a fuller understanding of all that is at play. It's a way of interrupting our automatic responses and living more intentionally to get the results that we really want in life, rather than the unsatisfying ones we've been getting.

In his book, *The Big Leap*, psychologist and author Gay Hendrix talks about what he calls the Upper-Limit problem, which is an inner thermostat that determines how much love, success, creativity, and wealth we will allow ourselves to have, based on the thermostat settings we programmed into our minds in childhood. This is no doubt the idea that Stephen Chbosky was getting at with the now famous quotation from his book (and one of my personal favorite novels) and subsequent film, *The Perks of Being a Wallflower*: "We accept the love we think we deserve."

Hendrix identifies hidden barriers that make up the anatomy of this self-limiting inner thermostat—each of which are only real when we make them real, since they are based on the false beliefs and fears based on how we view ourselves. Because the way we view ourselves becomes the reality we live into everyday, unearthing our self-perceptions and identifying their limiting nature becomes the pathway to freedom.

One common hidden barrier to be on the lookout for is the feeling that we're fundamentally flawed. This is related to the "I don't have what it takes" racket. It becomes an excuse to play small and not fully employ all of our gifts to accomplish our goals. We do this so that if we fail, we can tell ourselves that we didn't really put in that much effort, and if we had, then it would have worked out. We do this because we feel as though we would be devastated if we put in one hundred percent and then failed. We determine that that would mean we would be failures at the cores of who we are.

This is not true, of course, but the barrier becomes a protective mechanism, so that if we fail, the failure is on a much smaller scale—one that we could more quickly recover from. We know, though, that failure is only an event and not a person, and it is a necessary part of the path toward reaching our goals.

The barrier of feeling fundamentally flawed shows up in slightly more obscure ways as well. When I asked one of my clients if she'd be willing to make a request of her boss for a raise, she said to me, "Well, I'm still new at this job, so I'm kind of just blending into the crowd right now, not wanting to rock the boat." I gently reminded her that she'd been working there for over two years and asked how long she wanted to keep playing the "I'm new" card.

The concept of being "new" is another way of saying we feel unequipped, and we can drag this feeling out to last anywhere from a couple months to several years, so that we get to enjoy the payoffs of being expected to perform only at the level of a novice. These lowered expectations help us to feel safer, while continuing to play a much smaller, less inspiring game.

This also shows up as, "I'm just not ready yet," as if there were an objective way to be ready aside from simply deciding that we are ready and moving forward with the faith that we will be able to handle whatever comes our way. Asking ourselves, "Am I ready yet?" usually reveals fear, whereas the question, "Can I find the resources to take the next step toward reaching my goals?" tends to lead to a more productive mindset and greater possibilities.

The Capacity vs. Readiness distinction reminds me of a friend of mine who is a music producer, whom I'll call Jamal. Jamal and I worked on a music project together, during which he told me a story about how he got his start as a producer. He eventually became one of the top music producers in the industry, working with many of the biggest names in Hip-Hop and R&B.

Jamal was interested in producing, so as a teenager living in Atlanta, he spent a lot of his time in music studios shadowing up-and-coming music producers and also learning how to make beats on the drum machines himself, as a sort of internship. After some time he got the opportunity to work with a bigger name producer, helping out with beats and ideas for the Hip-Hop songs this producer was hired to work on. While he still wasn't making any money, he was learning what it was like to produce Hip-Hop records.

One day the executive producer of the project, whom I'll call Michael, sat in on one of the sessions and noticed that a lot of the ideas and beats that were being used for these Hip-Hop records were coming from Jamal, so Michael took Jamal aside later and asked him who was actually doing the lion-share of the work that was ending up on these albums. Jamal, of course, said that it was a group effort, grateful for the position he had and not wanting to throw anyone under the bus or lose his opportunity. Michael asked Jamal to meet him at his office the following day. Jamal agreed.

The next day he went to Michael's office and Michael told him that he was interested in creating a whole new style of music for outcast, fringe kids who were looking for a genre of music that would define them. Jamal, not having the slightest clue of how to do that, and only just beginning to understand the Hip-Hop world, responded confidently by saying, "Yeah, I could do that. No problem."

What Michael didn't know—aside from the fact that

Jamal didn't have any idea what he was doing and that he was simply an unpaid, temporary intern at the studio where they had met—was that Jamal was new to this whole music producing thing and didn't have any resources to speak of, even though he was putting up a bold front as if he were an established, albeit young, producer.

Jamal went home and did hours and hours of research and stayed up all night working on creating a new sound. He went back to Michael's office and the studio the next day and delivered what he had come up with. Michael liked it and took it to a major record label, which decided to sign and back the project.

Over the course of the next several weeks, Jamal would work in Michael's studio developing the sound and pretending to know about engineering and producing, as he taught himself along the way. One day, Michael was getting on Jamal's case about how certain tweaks needed to be made to the new tracks and how deadlines were surfacing. Jamal snapped and came clean.

"Look, I can't keep doing this! I have no money, and everyday I'm walking an hour and a half to work and an hour and a half home each night because I don't even have enough money for public transportation, and I've only got one pair of pants because the few clothes that I had got stolen from the laundromat. I have no food at home, and my mom's phone is shut off!"

Michael was taken aback. He had bought so much into Jamal's front—the front of him being an established producer with money—that he didn't think getting him paid right away was necessary. Jamal didn't want to blow his cover, so he never asked. Michael pulled a huge wad of cash out of his pocket, gave it to Jamal, and said, "Go now, and buy yourself some clothes, get your family some food, and get your mom's phone turned back on. Then come back tomorrow and we'll work everything else out."

Jamal did just that and came back the next day. That day Michael told Jamal what his weekly base salary would be—which was more money than Jamal had ever seen in his life—and how much he would give him for every track he produced. Jamal's bank account went from zero to hundreds of thousands of dollars within a few short months, and more than that, his career as a music producer was launched.

He understood the distinction between being ready and believing that he had the capacity to find the resources he would need to get the job done. He could have easily talked himself out of the game and admitted that he wasn't ready, but that safe route could have cost him so much.

The distinction between capacity and readiness could also be seen as the distinction between capacity and confidence. We often back down when we don't feel confident, but instead we could ask ourselves, "Do I have the capacity to figure it out?" And the answer is nearly always, "Yes." Confidence can be elusive, since it's often based on mood, or how we feel in a certain outfit, or what big wins we've recently had, and so on. This wavering feeling of confidence can't always be counted on, but believing in our capacity can be a firmer foundation. It's a place where we can naturally come from, not a place we need to get to, like confidence can often be.

One other important note about Jamal's story is something he said to me recently while reflecting on his journey. He said that the reason he took on that seemingly impossible task was out of desperation. There was a sense of urgency that was driving him. Many people get stuck and lose out on opportunity after opportunity because of the thought that there is plenty of time to get after the things we want in life. Instead of instilling some sort of time-sensitive system or self-imposed desperation, we put it off and put it off until eventually another decade has passed along with an infinite amount of opportunities down the drain, telling ourselves we just didn't have time. As author Robert J. Hastings says, "The great dividing line between success and failure can be expressed in five words: 'I did not have time.'"

Another barrier to look out for is the fear of upstaging others. This limiting voice says that if I go after and begin to reach what I'm capable of attaining, then I'll outshine someone else and make them feel bad. High achievers are particularly susceptible to this underlying belief. They learn early on that their gifts and achievements are not always met with praise but often with jealousy and exclusion. So the unconscious response to such alienation is often one

I CAN'T GET BEYOND THIS CEILING

or both of two options: pull back on our accomplishments or pull back on the enjoyment of those accomplishments.

The problem here is that nobody is inspired by us when we play small, and the world misses out on potentially tremendous services and resources when we choose to play it safe instead of playing to win and win big. The primary way lives are transformed by others is through inspiration, and inspiration generally comes as a result of how we're living.

If some are discouraged by our success, that's okay; they're not yet at a place where they view life abundantly; they are living in a small world where the success of others means less for everybody else. This is not objectively true; it is simply a perception that success is a limited resource, and we have to fight for what is ours.

In contrast to the scarcity of limited resources, such as wealth or food, there is no upper limit to the accomplishment of dreams; thus, there is no reason for competition, greed, or envy to arise as a result of another's accomplishments.

One additional barrier that I've noticed in my clients who would classify themselves as people of faith is that success, and especially financial wealth, is unspiritual, whereas a lower income is a greater expression of humility or meekness. Now, I'm not interested in arguing whether this is true or false, only that we recognize that these beliefs may be in play and thus are part of our realities. Once we see

YOUR PROSPEROUS MIND / **Racketeering**

that, we can make more authentic decisions about whether we want to continue adhering to these beliefs or if we'd rather adopt a different mindset—something that may be more resourceful for us and the world around us.

One of my clients reframed this belief by getting clear about where he wanted to spend his money. He made it his goal to give a million dollars to his faith community, who used their funds to dig wells and provide fresh water where it was previously unavailable; free women from sexual slavery; and feed, clothe, and educate those in abject poverty. This isn't the path for everyone, but once we get clear on the beliefs driving our behavior, we can choose to hold onto them or replace them with new commitments or declarations.

I've talked a lot in this chapter about patterns of thought and behavior that stem from childhood, which is where many of our chosen behaviors originate. This doesn't mean we need to spend years digging and discovering all the events and conversations that lead to the limiting voices and beliefs that we've adopted and why we adhere to them. Discovering the "why" for each of our belief systems may be interesting (and certainly helpful as it relates to understanding the purposes of the rackets and the payoffs of certain behaviors), but it's not critical as it relates to having the future you want.

I'm not saying that counseling and therapy don't have value; they absolutely do. A lot of healing can take place through therapy, which I went through and benefited from for a few years myself. But in the meantime, we can be in action, staying in the moment, which is the only place we can create beautiful futures to live into.

As we come up against resistance and barriers, it is often a great resource to find out which rackets and limiting beliefs are at play and choose to be aware of them while remaining steadfast toward our commitments.

If any of the barriers or limiting thoughts mentioned in this chapter connected with you, or if a different one came to mind, write it down and ask yourself how it might be limiting your potential. Examine this limiting voice and see if there might be evidence that negates this belief and would support a worldview that would be more resourceful in attaining your dreams.

9

I'm Frustrated

"Acceptance doesn't mean resignation;
it means understanding that something is what it is
and that there's got to be a way through it."
~MICHAEL J. FOX

As we've said, success in any endeavor comes from staying on the path toward your vision, and one of the most common stuck places for people is frustration.

Frustration (a code word for anger) is essentially a resistance to current reality. This resistance has a tendency to produce more of whatever we're resisting, because what we dwell on grows in intensity. The things to which we give our attention and energy gain power and momentum as we choose to make them important to us. Carl Jung, the founder of analytical psychology, says, "What you resist, persists." The more consciousness we give to a certain thought, the more real it becomes to us. And when we choose to believe that the thought is true, it further impacts our lives and occurs to us as an obstacle or a problem.

This is why mere positive thinking, simply trying to replace negative thoughts with positive ones, tends to blow up in our faces. This addresses the "problem" as something that needs to be avoided, as a *problem*. As soon as we see these negative thoughts as a problem, as something that needs to be gotten rid of or replaced, it occurs to us as a real thing—as something powerful that needs to be resisted. And this, in turn, increases its power over us. The truth is that negative thoughts will pop into our minds all day long, and we can choose to entertain them as truth, or we can investigate and interrogate them in order to see whether they really line up with reality.

We create the *meaning* of these problems. When we think about the issue we're frustrated with, it's not the issue itself that is frustrating us. Instead, it's the thoughts and beliefs about it that we're entertaining.

For example, if I'm frustrated with a friend who is not following through on his end of the deal for a collaborative project we're working on, it's not his lack of action that is frustrating me; rather, what makes me crazy are my thoughts about it, like, "This shouldn't be happening. This is bad for me. This project is never actually going to get completed. He's always this way. Why do I attract these types of people in my life? I'm never going to reach the dreams I've set out to accomplish." Once our minds start down this road, frustration mounts. We think we're frustrated with the circumstance or the person, when really our frustration comes from what we choose to think and believe about the situation. As Greek Stoic philosopher Epictetus says, "Men are disturbed, not by things, but by the principles and notions which they form concerning things."

Fortunately, we have a million other options concerning which thoughts we can think and make real for ourselves. Don't resist the old thoughts or try to replace them with new ones by force; instead create a new set of thoughts without demonizing the old ones. Greek philosopher Socrates says, "The secret of change is to focus all of your energy, not on fighting the old, but on building the new."

One new set of thoughts I can focus my energy on would be: "I've been avoiding having a 'tough' conversation with him for a while and haven't spoken up in the past when this has happened. Since I've taken part in creating this situation through my avoidance of conflict, I also have the power to create something different. I would like to create an agreement with him and have a closer relationship in which conflicting thoughts and ideas are no longer scary to me but are welcome." This is the mindset of a creator rather than someone who is simply reacting, like a victim.

You see, frustration is most often not only a resistance to current reality but also a replacement for change and creation. It is a choice, and that choice comes at the expense of a new vision. Resistance takes energy and focus away from the new vision, so instead of asking ourselves what we'd like to create in light of our circumstances, we remain stuck in the purgatory of wishing things were different. It then becomes a racket that allows us to stay safe and stuck, avoiding the work it would take to create a new path or opportunity, which is well within our power to do.

The irony is that this circumstance—the "problem"—almost always has a gift in it that will benefit us while creating a new vision. The "problem" itself is actually encapsulating the opportunity that we so desperately desire. That opportunity often comes in the form of *growth*, and growth is one of the primary sources of happiness in this life.

Frustration is also an avoidance tactic—and avoidance is another way to resist progress—that is connected to a forecasting of the future. For example, let's say your car has been making a funny noise or is driving strangely or the engine light illuminates. This has been going on for some time now. Every time you get into your car you feel frustrated and upset, thinking to yourself, "I *just know* this is going to cost a thousand dollars or more to fix, and I don't have that kind of money lying around right now." And then that reminds you that you hate your job and don't make enough money, which leads to a feeling of sorrow and some self-loathing, which leads to further avoidance of the car problem.

This happens in relationships all the time, too. Let's say I feel frustrated that a project isn't moving forward, and I'm waiting to hear back from a key person. If I don't watch myself, I'll begin to assume what's going on with that person and think, "They haven't gotten back to me, which probably means that they hate me, don't want to work with me, and think that I don't have anything of value to offer." So then maybe I'll avoid that project until "later," which likely means I'll avoid it indefinitely.

When feeling frustrated with a person, we tend to avoid them and make up stories about why it's useless to have a conversation about the grievance. We might say, "Oh, we've been through this before. I don't want to get into it right now. I'll say this, and he'll say that, and then I'll say this, and then we'll be in the same place as before, but then things will be awkward, so I'll just leave it alone and try to forget about it."

Each of the frustrations that we hold onto in our lives takes up a certain amount of bandwidth in our minds, making our lives feel more overwhelming and chaotic. So the more we resist and avoid, the more difficult it becomes to focus on the projects we care about or think creatively about them.

What frustrations are you holding onto right now? What situations are you resisting? Where is there a lack of peace in your life? In light of the reality of a circumstance that feels negative to you, what would you like to create? What kind of relationship would you like to create with someone you're frustrated with? What new vision, goal, or plan would you like to establish in light of your frustration?

You will be amazed by how much peace, creativity, and vitality rushes into you once the resistance stops and the creation begins. Resistance takes up so much bandwidth in the brain. On the other side of that resistance you will often find freedom, opportunity, and success.

The step between resistance and creation, of course, is acceptance. The quicker we can get connected to current realities and accept a situation for what it is, the faster we can get out of breakdown and back into action toward what we want to create.

In her book, *Loving What Is*, author Byron Katie says, "I am a lover of what is, not because I'm a spiritual person, but because it hurts when I argue with reality." Those in Alcoholics Anonymous and other twelve step programs understand this principle too as they have adopted theologian Reinhold Niebuhr's prayer, often referred to as the Serenity Prayer: "God, grant me the serenity to accept the things I cannot change, the courage to change the things I can, and the wisdom to know the difference."

What are the areas of resistance in your life right now? In light of those circumstances, what would you like to create for yourself and for those you love? Acceptance isn't a weak, resigned stance; it's a launching point toward the beautiful future that you're creating.

10

Fantasy

"We live in a fantasy world, a world of illusion.
The great task in life is to find reality."
~IRIS MURDOCH

Picture this: I'm thirteen years old, I weigh 86 pounds, and I throw my arms into the air and say, "Why don't you say it to my face?!" This, in retrospect, didn't make any sense, because the guy hadn't actually *said* anything about me.

Let me back up and give you some context. My buddy Ray and I were at Raging Waters, a water park in San Dimas, California, and we were walking from one end of the park to the next when—"Ouch!"—I felt a stinging pain on the back of my shoulder. I looked on the ground just behind me and noticed a piece of a churro—you know, those cinnamon sugary pastries?

So, I looked over in the direction that the sugary missile came from and noticed a group of teens laughing. This hurt my teenaged, angsty ego, so I threw my arms up in the air and said, "Why don't you say it to my face?!"

The adolescents all looked to be about my age, maybe a year or two older, and most were about as scrawny as I was…except for one of them. All of a sudden, this muscle-bound Neanderthal emerged from the teens and started thundering toward me.

I could feel a bead of sweat roll down my face, as I regretted shooting off my big mouth. But I was determined to stand my ground. The jacked teen got right in my face and stared at me. I stared at him. He stared at me. I stared at him. He stared at me. And eventually, he walked away. *Ha! Victory was mine.* As he walked away I said, still cocky as hell, "That's what I thought."

My buddy Ray, who hadn't done anything to help the situation, by the way, was still standing next to me. I looked over at him, and he said urgently, "Dude, are you okay?!" And I said, "Yeah, of course. What are you talking about? Didn't you see what just happened? I scared the dude off." Ray looked at me in disbelief and said, "No, that's not what happened. He punched you in the face, hard. And you just stood there looking stupid for so long that he eventually walked away."

So, why am I telling you this humiliating story? Because sometimes what I think is happening is not actually happening. Sometimes I'm living in fantasy, outside of reality. And the worst part is that this is not just an isolated case or something that only happened when I was a kid. This is happening in just about every sphere of my life, even now. And worse than that, I often don't even realize it's going on.

The above is an example of how I live in fantasy in a way that makes me perceive myself as greater than I truly am, when my ego gets the best of me. This falls in line with what author and psychiatrist, Dr. William Glasser says: "Our view of ourselves ranges from flattery to pure fantasy."

There is another way that I can often live in fantasy, and that is believing I am less than I truly am—dumber, less capable, unworthy, and so on. Historically, this has been the case when I'm in the midst of a new pursuit. Currently my newest pursuit is acting. Somehow there is a disconnect in my mind between my actual ability and my perceived ability. No matter how much I train, and I train a lot, I most often walk around with a sense that I suck, that I'm not enough, and that I don't (and won't) have what it takes to succeed as a professional actor.

I'm using the word "fantasy" here to refer to the ways we live outside of reality, whether we would consider it "positive" or "negative" fantasy. An example of a "negative" fantasy is having an unrealistically low opinion of ourselves and what we're capable of accomplishing. On the flip side, a "positive" fantasy is believing we're superheroes, for instance. Whether positive or negative, fantasies create a gap, a disconnect between what we perceive to be happening and what is actually happening.

For example, have you ever said or done something that somebody misunderstood, and later found out that it hurt or offended them in some way? I'm guessing that when you found out you offended them, you thought, or maybe even said to the person, "Well, that's not what I meant," or, "That wasn't my *intention.*"

In my first book, *The Voice of Your Dreams*, I talked about the difference between *intention* and *impact*, which I want to re-visit here from a slightly different angle.

You see, when intention doesn't align with impact, we're living in fantasy. In the scenario in which you were misunderstood, your intention (or intended impact) may have been to make people laugh or maybe even to help someone through instruction or constructive criticism. But the impact was offense and hurt feelings. There was a gap between the intention and the impact. And the degree that we have this disconnect in any area of our lives is the degree to which we are living in some sort of fantasy. Recognizing this gap would snap us back into reality, of course, but I'm getting a little ahead of myself.

Okay, so what? So what if we're all living in fantasy in many areas of our lives? What's the harm? Isn't this just part of life?

Here's the thing: when we live in fantasy we lose traction toward our intended goals. The more we live in reality, the faster we can move toward the results that we want in our lives.

For example, when I first decided I wanted to seriously pursue acting I was under the delusion that acting is simply a matter of talent—you either had it or you didn't. I had done quite of bit of acting and performing as a kid and throughout my life, so I just figured it was simply a matter of getting the right opportunity or getting my "big break." While this certainly does happen from time to time, the reality is that an overnight success is most often ten, fifteen, twenty years in the making. It comes to the ones who train in the craft for many, many years. This is true for all artistic pursuits.

Once this really sunk in for me, I began training with some of the best acting coaches in L.A., practicing for several hours a day, week after week, month after month. And, not surprisingly, I've now begun to book my first professional roles: a couple commercials, a TV show, and a film. Reality gave me traction, because it gave me clarity on what I could do to begin reaching my goals. It helped me realize that mastery over an artistic craft is a life-long pursuit. I understood this to be the case with playing guitar and singing, but somehow thought it might be different with acting. I was wrong. That was a fantasy.

So, if it's true that confronting reality allows us to accomplish our goals faster, then why do we live in fantasy so often and in so many areas of our lives?

In the above story about my 13-year-old self—and really whenever one's ego is running the show—fantasy is a way to comfort and shield myself from what I perceive may be a painful reality. Living in fantasy gives us the illusion of safety.

On the other hand, when I live outside of reality by believing I'm capable of *less* than I really am, I'm allowing myself to play small—playing to avoid losing rather than playing to win. It's a racket that gives me an excuse to not go all-in for the pursuit because, "What's the point, if it's never going to work out anyway?" It's a way to feel complacent about quitting or only putting in a half-hearted effort toward our pursuits—especially those pursuits that scare us, the ones that produce a sense of inadequacy or a fear of failure.

The good news is that there is a clear, simple, but not always easy way to close the gap between our intentions and our impacts by releasing the fantasy and getting face-to-face with reality. The quickest way to do this is to seek feedback.

For our purposes, I'm defining feedback as others' experiences or opinions of our actions, attitudes, and products. It's an outside perspective on who you are and what you create—or, in other words, your impact. So, the function of feedback is to allow you to evaluate the disconnect between your intent and your impact. And the gap between intent and impact equals reality.

The problem with feedback, though, is that it can be disruptive to one's ego or self-perception. Because we benefit from the complacency of living in fantasy, feed-back's attempt to snap us back to reality brings with it a little bit of whiplash. For example, I was benefiting plenty from believing that success as an actor was more about being discovered than about a constant pursuit of mastery in the craft: I was off the hook from training hard daily. I could complain that it's all about who you know. I could believe that I was a genius and savant who was just under-appreciated. Living in a fantasy world, indeed.

This is why seeking and accepting feedback is so vital. Most often we sit in our fantasies and have no idea how laughable our belief systems really are. It would be funny if it weren't so destructive to the future we're seeking to create.

We have a couple different options when it comes to accepting feedback. The first is to take it personally, freak out, and grip onto the fantasy that we've created even more tightly. This is the option I choose more often than I'd like to admit.

For example, after I wrote the initial draft of my first book, *The Voice of Your Dreams*, for which I had done my first couple rounds of edits, I then sent it out to a substantial list of beta readers for feedback. I gave them a list of things I wanted them to do: tell me when you rolled your eyes, tell me when you got bored and went on Facebook, tell me a section you hated, tell me a section you loved, and so on.

I got one piece of feedback that really delivered a blow. One reader I really respect said that while he liked the majority of the actual principles and content, he felt that the stories I told about my successes lacked vulnerability and authenticity. Additionally, my stories were missing the failures and stumbling blocks I experienced along the way.

This feedback was painfully and embarrassingly valid. I had the choice to take it personally or take it as constructive feedback. I could have made the necessary changes without throwing myself a pity party and letting the "You Suck" voice dominate my mind. In this particular case I chose the latter—I saw this feedback as a deathblow.

You see, what I heard him say is, "You don't understand storytelling. You're not skilled enough to be writing a book at all. You need to learn a lot more to be able to do this successfully." My interpretation of this feedback sent me into a self-loathing spiral for a couple of weeks before I decided to really appreciate the feedback and begin making changes accordingly. I spent nearly a month doing rewrites for just that one piece of feedback. And the book was a much better product as a result. In fact, the most common feedback I receive about the completed book is how pleasantly surprised people are with how raw and vulnerable the storytelling is. It's become one of the very things for which the book is known.

Taking feedback personally often causes us to demonize the person who provided the feedback. We tear them down in our minds to justify why their feedback is irrelevant and unfounded. This is also the path to stagnation. It's nearly impossible to grow when we're unwilling to take feedback and make changes accordingly.

Taking feedback is a form of learning. And the challenge with learning is that it's always an affront to our egos. As psychiatrist and psychoanalyst Thomas Szasz says, "Every act of conscious learning requires the willingness to suffer an injury to one's self-esteem. That is why young children, before they are aware of their own self-importance, learn so easily." So, when we fight against feedback, we are essentially believing the lie that we already know everything we need to know. And again, growth stops in its tracks right there.

Take some time to write down a few areas that may be fantasy pitfalls for you. In the following chapter, we'll talk about some practical ways to pinpoint fantasies and align ourselves with reality.

11

Reality

"There are some people who live in a dream world,
and there are some who face reality;
and then there are those who turn one into the other."
~Desiderius Erasmus

In the previous chapter we said that one of the most effective ways of connecting with reality is receiving feedback. So, what are some actual ways to receive the feedback we need to pursue our visions, goals, and dreams?

The most obvious way to get feedback is to simply ask for it directly, as I did with my beta readers for my first book. Just as I did, you can even give them specific guidelines for the types of feedback you're seeking. If you're working on a specific project like mine, it can be pretty straightforward to ask for and receive feedback.

But with other areas in our lives it may not be so cut and dried. Remember, we said that there are many different areas in our lives where we are living in fantasy, and we most often don't even realize it. This is a big deal because it's very difficult to make progress when you don't even know where the progress needs to be made.

The good news is that in these more elusive areas, there are generally little red flags that help us notice where we're living in fantasy. One of those red flags is tension.

There are different types of tension. The good type of tension is the tension between where we currently are and where we ultimately hope to be. That never really goes away, because as soon as we reach one goal, we reset the clock and set our aims on the next dream or vision.

One warning sign that we're living in fantasy is the tension caused by avoiding something like a task or a conversation. Active avoidance means that there are some unexamined thoughts or beliefs that have transformed into fantasy.

If there is unaddressed tension in your relationship with a family member, the unconscious story you might be telling yourself is, "If I ignore it it'll go away," or, "It'll work itself out," or, "If I open that can of worms it'll only serve to make things worse rather than better." Or you may have a different set of stories, like, "He doesn't approve of some decisions I've made, so it's better if I just cut off communication," or, "I know exactly how she's going to respond, and trust me, it won't do any good to bring it up."

Avoiding tasks often brings up the more classic fantasy narratives, like, "It'll never work out," or, "They're going to say 'no' anyway, so I'll save myself the humiliation," or simply, "I don't have what it takes to succeed in that endeavor."

And again, rather than engage, get real world feedback, and suffer some failures, we often allow our fantasy narratives to keep us on the sidelines without fully realizing the source of our stagnation—our own constructed narratives.

Another way to get feedback is learning from failure. Failure is feedback.

In my previous book I wrote about my gargantuan failure with my initial online singing lesson program, that I, at the time, called "The Singing Guide" (TSG). I'm not even sure you could actually give it the honor of calling it a failure. It seems that you have to at least have a single sale to be a failure, whereas TSG had zero. It was more of a non-starter, even though I had spent two years developing it and had a "big" launch. In retrospect, the reason TSG was a massive failure is a little clearer now than it was at the time.

If you have any connection with the tech industry you've probably heard the phrase "Minimum Viable Product" (MVP). The MVP is a way for a company to mitigate risk. The company creates a product, like an app, for instance, and spends as little time, money, and resources as possible to get a workable product complete. Once they have the MVP of their product, they send it out to a sample of the intended audience (beta users or a beta test group) to review it and give feedback about how functional it is, whether the market is ready for it, and whether there might be bugs. So rather than bet the farm on something they're not sure is going to fly, they start smaller. If the feedback suggests that they're ready to move onto the next step, they pour a lot more time and resources into the product and eventually do a full launch.

This is exactly what we did *not* do with TSG, which is probably one of the primary reasons it was a flop. We didn't seek out any feedback that would have aligned us with reality and helped us to see what it might take to create a product that would really help and connect with people. Instead, we received feedback in the form of failure—a harsh reality check.

I did eventually use that feedback of failure to seek out more specific feedback from others, which led to lots of tweaking, studying, rebranding, re-filming, and renaming the program that is now Superior Singing Method. We then launched it again about one year later and the impact was, and continues to be, strong.

Another great way to get feedback is through coaching. The primary goal of coaching is to provide feedback. Being a coach myself, I would be remiss not to mention the potential power of bold, fearless, direct feedback that is available from a great coach.

One of the primary purposes of a coach, from my vantage point, is to listen to the language of a client. Hearing their language gives insight into their worldview. The stories they're telling themselves about who they are and the world around them demonstrate whether they're living outside of reality, in some sort of fantasy. Once I have this information I can give them feedback and help them realign their perspectives with reality, so that they can gain traction toward more radical results in their lives.

For example, while coaching one of my clients, whom I'll call Louie, I could hear one of the stories he was telling himself. He was making a decent living and running a million-dollar business but knew he could have a much greater impact if he had more income. But he had some latent beliefs that were keeping him from doing so. As we explored some of those belief systems we discovered that there was some part of him that believed that money was evil. Being a person of faith, he had believed that somehow poverty was connected to spirituality and the more money you have, the less spiritual you are.

So we began to take a very detailed look at all the things he would do with money if he had it. We took an arbitrary number, two million dollars, and mapped out all the things he would do if he had that kind of surplus. He was already doing great work serving underrepresented groups of people, and he wanted to continue serving them with an increased surplus. As he began to really see the good that could come out of having more resources, his mind began to shift from these false beliefs that he had held dear for so long.

He is still a client of mine, and his company is currently worth two million dollars, and with the business that he already has lined up, the company's projected worth is three million dollars by the end of the year.

Another one of my clients, whom I'll call Jessica, was living outside of reality in regard to relationships. When we first started working together Jessica hadn't dated anyone for 14 years but really wanted to be married and start a family. With some exploration I discovered that she had two conflicting beliefs that were keeping her stuck. Because of some experiences Jessica had when she was younger, she developed the belief that all men were dangerous and not to be trusted. Her other belief was that she wouldn't be truly fulfilled if she was not in a loving relationship with a man.

Jessica was living in a fantasy about relationships that wasn't prevented her from getting traction in her personal life. Once we discovered this and began to really question her beliefs, she discovered that both of these beliefs were false—not all men were dangerous, and she could live a beautifully fulfilling life with or without a spouse.

After confronting these false beliefs, Jessica began to see herself and her relationships much differently. And as a result, Jessica is currently in a committed relationship that is heading toward marriage.

Living in reality is powerful. It gives us traction toward our goals. We're often afraid to look behind the curtain to see reality because we think that what we find will be too scary—that it will be worse than the fantasy we're living in.

My wife and I facilitate financial workshops where we help people get out of debt, begin budgeting, and increase their wealth. And we find over and over again that people avoid budgeting and really taking a hard look at their finances out of fear of what they might find. But inevitably, no matter how bad their financial situation is, it's never as bad as they thought it might be. And even if it is bad, they now have a grasp on reality and know what they need to do to get things straightened out.

The same is true for any area of our lives. As scary as reality may seem, it's almost never as bad as we think it is. And more than that, we have what it takes to set things right more often than we think we do.

If living in reality is much more likely to lead us to our goals and desires in life, then why don't we confront reality more often and in more areas of our lives?

Well, for me, I tend to believe the lie that fantasy is more fun. I often like to live in the story that tells me I'm the hero, I'm never wrong, and everybody loves me. Or I like to milk the pity that comes from seeing myself as a victim.

It can feel very vulnerable to live in reality. Because in reality, the relationship may need work; in reality, the business may need to be shut down; in reality, you may need to train for a few more years before you're ready to truly compete with others in your industry. But nobody wants to hear or believe that—there are certainly plenty of times when I don't.

But reality is our friend because it tells us where we actually are, and it's very difficult to get to where we want to go without knowledge of where we're starting.

Take a moment to write down three areas in your life that you would like to have better results in. It could be in relationships, finances, business, dreams, or whatever it is you want to improve. Then ask yourself how you can get some feedback that will help you confront reality, so that you can begin to create a future worth living into.

PART IV

INCREASED PRODUCTIVITY

12

Am I In Breakdown?

"Responsibility is the price of freedom."
~ELBERT HUBBARD

When we feel stuck in any area of our lives, it's usually an indicator that we're in breakdown. We know that we're in breakdown from the feedback we're getting from reality. If there's tension in our relationships or we're not moving toward the realization of our dreams or our bank accounts are much smaller than we'd like them to be, for example, then we're in breakdown.

Anytime anything in life isn't working, that is, when our current reality is not in alignment with the vision we have for that particular area of our lives, we're in breakdown. At any given time we can be in breakdowns in multiple parts of our lives. And there's no shame in this. Left unattended, our lives can move quite naturally into breakdown. The problem isn't necessarily the fact that our lives drift into breakdown; the problem comes when we don't recognize it and stay stuck there for hours, days, months, or years. We have the ability to get out of breakdown almost immediately and get back on the path toward a successful relationship or business or artistic goal.

Of course we can't always get all the results we want *immediately*, but we can get back on the path toward those results, and it's staying on the path that leads us to success.

The *first* thing to do to get out of breakdown is identify that there is a breakdown. Without a focused awareness that something isn't working and that there is a clear way to get back on the path, we tend to have this nagging sense that things just can't work. We feel down and maybe depressed or angry but aren't really sure why. It just feels like a nebulous sense that the world is pressing in on us.

Once we clearly define what the breakdown is, then we can pool together all of our faculties and resources and figure out a way to move forward. One powerful way to do this is to write it down. Once we can see where the breakdown is, by articulating it we put ourselves in a more resourceful place to understand it. But as long as the situation remains foggy, it continues to feel huge and scary and unmanageable.

I spent my third year of graduate school working on my master's thesis, which was called "Adolescent Boys' Use of (Emo) Music as a Healing Lament." Throughout my time working on the thesis, and simultaneously working with youth, I discovered that a large part of adolescent suffering (and I don't believe this is exclusive to teenagers) stems from a type of pain that is unnamed. It's not that the suffering can't be named, but until we can find language for it, it seems impossible to pinpoint and therefore impossible to shake.

If we can find language for this pain, and subsequently the source of it, then the angsty feeling loses some of its power, and it begins to occur to us differently, as something that is more manageable. This suffering— or unhappiness or stress—could stem from something as simple as an awkward conversation, or something much more complex like a bankruptcy or a divorce. Either way, this principle applies.

There is something about writing the problem or breakdown on a piece of paper that pulls it out of our minds and allows us to the see it as finite. It feels more manageable once we can look at it and see that the real problem is the story we're telling ourselves and much less the circumstance itself.

In the thesis I talk about how artists—poets, singers, songwriters—have a way of articulating suffering that we can grab onto and use to articulate what's going on inside of us. Famous composer, conductor, and author Leonard Bernstein says, "Music can name the unnameable and communicate the unknowable." Articulating our feelings, whether through music or any other outlet, allows us to take the next step toward freedom.

The *second* thing to do to get out of breakdown is take responsibility for it. This doesn't necessarily mean that breakdown is one hundred percent your fault, but the more responsibility you take for it, the more power of choice returns to you in the present moment.

We usually associate taking responsibility with accepting blame. But if we could shift our understanding and see taking responsibility as a way to take control over the things we want in our lives, real transformations could take place inside of us.

We can begin to accept responsibility by asking ourselves questions like, "How did I contribute to creating this?" or, "What could I have done differently?" This line of questioning takes us out of the victim mindset and back into the driver's seat, where we have the power to effect change.

Recognize the tendency here to jump into a shame racket and start beating yourself up, which is why the *third* step to getting out of breakdown is to forgive yourself. If necessary, this is the time to forgive others as well.

The more you take ownership of the breakdown, the less there will be to forgive others for. If you can take one hundred percent of the responsibility, I highly recommend it. Let it occur to you differently, as if the more responsibility you take, the more power you now have. It's simply more resourceful to reframe mistakes of the past and see them as tools rather than indictments.

Forgiving oneself is often harder for people than forgiving others. A certain feeling of pseudo-strength arises when we give into shame. It's tricky to avoid, too, because we feel as if shame comes upon us from the outside, but the reality is that we choose shame because of the pay-offs we get from it—just like any other racket. Author and shame researcher Brené Brown, in her book *Daring Greatly*, defines shame as "the intensely painful feeling or experience of believing that we are flawed and therefore unworthy of love and belonging."

It's a little different for everyone, but I know that when I choose shame I get to justify continuing shameful behavior because, "What's the use? All is lost anyway." When I indulge in feelings of shame I get to feel self-righteous about the fact that I'm now punishing myself with a sort of mental self-flagellation. I also get to isolate myself and avoid any type of accountability because, "Can't you see I'm already beating myself up? How dare you call me out?"

There are a lot of reasons we choose shame, but it will never lead us back onto a resourceful path toward our goals. In fact, living in shame is a way of living in the past, which by very definition is a stuck place that prevents us from laying the groundwork for a beautiful future.

So after we've forgiven ourselves, the *fourth* thing to do to get out of breakdown is to make a new commitment, or create a new vision. Ask yourself, "In light of the current circumstances, what would I like to create? What would I like to commit to that would give me a future worth living into?"

Having a clear idea of our visions—of what we want next—is a major step toward getting out of the funk and back onto the path toward our goals. If we can create that clear vision of and commitment to what we want, then we have something to live into besides regret.

In what ways are you experiencing breakdown now? Are you willing to take few moments to think about it? Once you identify the area(s) of concern, walk it through the breakdown structure, and see how you feel afterward.

Steps for Getting Out of Breakdown

Identify breakdown

- What's not working?
- Where are my actions misaligned with my vision?
- Where do I want clearer direction in my life?

Take responsibility

- How did I contribute to this breakdown?
- If I added more consciousness to this area, could I better understand how I contributed to this breakdown?
- How might I have created this or even wanted it?

Forgive yourself

- I choose to let myself off the hook for this.
- Each day and each moment have a fresh dose of mercy available to me.
- I choose to speak kindly to myself and avoid shame.

Make a new vision

- In light of my current circumstances, what would I like to create?
- To what end goal would I like to commit myself?
- What do I really want in this area that I don't currently have?

13

Sorry I'm Late

"Integrity is when what you think
is the same as what you say,
and when what you say
is the same as what you do."
~Mahatma Gandhi

One of my primary goals with my coaching clients, for life coaching and vocal coaching, is to help them build up this muscle called commitment. Because when it is strengthened it becomes a superhero-like power. This is true for accomplishing goals, strengthening relationships, and creating wealth.

Most people break commitments all day long and don't even realize it. I usually start small with my clients. I start at the same place my coach started with me—punctuality.

At first this might seem like a trivial issue that's just a part of our culture, so who really cares, right? But how we do one thing is often an indicator of how we do everything. Our words and actions in the minutia of daily life reveal a belief system and a way of being that tend to infiltrate most, if not all, areas of our lives. And, to further the point, these small broken commitments usually reveal an attitude or preference of which we may not even be fully aware.

For example, I recently started working with a new coaching client who was fifteen minutes late to our first coaching session. He said that he had gotten called in for work unexpectedly that day, and while he was actually still home in plenty of time to be on time for the call, he was thrown off and "confused" by this change in schedule and "forgot" about our phone session until fifteen minutes after our scheduled time.

The following week he was one minute late for our second session. And even though it was only a small infraction, it revealed a pattern to me, so I pressed him. I asked if he was aware that we had a broken commitment, given that he had made a promise to be on time—down to the minute—to every session. He was "confused" at first and didn't see what I was getting at, but as I continued to dig deeper, he admitted that he didn't like being told what to do (who does, right?), and he was concerned that that's what coaching would look like.

Once I explained to him that that wasn't how coaching worked, and that my job was to listen to what he wants— to help him get unstuck from where he was and get the results he wanted in life—his fear faded. Then we were able to move forward from there. He's never been late to a session since then.

So let's take a look at what was going on underneath the surface. His fear, which came from a belief that he had made up, revealed itself in a broken commitment. This happens all the time. A broken commitment is most often a cry for help.

In this case there was something my new client needed of which he was only partially aware, so he began to sabotage himself as well as our coaching relationship without realizing what he was doing. He blamed it on forgetfulness or confusion, which are very common self-betraying rackets.

When we don't take the time to check in with ourselves and see what we're really feeling and what we really want, forgetfulness and confusion are often the go-to smokescreens.

Likewise, if we are more self-aware and know exactly what we want but are too fearful to have a conversation about it, we will often continue to choose forgetfulness and confusion as excuses. We may break commitments until another person eventually initiates the conversation, or the relationship with that person dissolves completely.

That's the thing about broken commitments, big or small. They *always* have an immediate impact on the person who is on the receiving end of the broken promise. When we say we'll do something and then we don't, we plant a seed of distrust in the other person and the foundation of the relationship, whether personal or professional, becomes shaky. Things begin to fall apart from there, because the very foundation of every relationship is trustworthiness.

The fulfillment of a commitment is revealed in what we actually do, not what we intend to do or say we'll do. Once we've taken action, we know that we've followed through on a commitment. This is living in integrity—living with a sense of wholeness.

This is important as it relates to getting the things we want in life. It's true that relationships and the trust of others can break down when we break commitments, and thus lack integrity, but there is another level to this as well. When we get used to breaking commitments, we begin to not trust ourselves. When we break our commitments to ourselves enough times, the language we use loses its power to create new futures. Our language is relegated to being descriptive rather than generative, no longer utilizing all of its potential power.

Generative language, the kind of language that has the power to alter our lives and our futures, is intimately connected to the idea of commitment, of following through with what we say we'll do. Generative language produces results in our lives when we put ourselves at risk with investments of time and energy, much like our money is at risk when we invest it into the stock market.

Some examples of generative, declarative language that we can use are, "I'm going to finish writing a book by July 31st," or, "I'm committed to showing up ten minutes early to all of my engagements this week," or, "I'm committed to inspire others when they're around me." Without the commitment or follow-through on what we say we'll do, our language can only be used to describe, with statements like, "I feel sad," or, "I have brown hair," or "I hope things change." This is all that's possible when we cease to believe our own words and commitments. We always have the choice to use generative language, which opens up possibility, or descriptive language, which is useful for reading a map or menu but not for opening up new opportunities. Descriptive language implies that reality "is what it is" and won't or can't change.

If I don't believe that I'll follow through with what I say I'm going to do anymore because of all my broken commitments to myself and others, then when I commit to, say, writing a book, I don't ever get started on it. I think to myself, "I never really follow through on what I say; why would I think this time would be any different, especially for an undertaking as big as this?"

The impact of a broken commitment is not only the mistrust of others, but also a decrease of confidence in ourselves and our abilities to create change in our lives. We bring that mistrust of ourselves into every endeavor and every relationship, tainting them from the very beginning.

So it's no wonder that our lives seem cyclical, like we're getting the same unwanted results over and over again no matter what we read or what seminars we go to or which classes we take or how hard we work.

Acknowledge that making a decision to commit to something is just that—a decision, a choice. No matter what we've chosen in the past, we have the ability to make new choices, starting now. We're not broken because we've made habits of breaking commitments; it's not "just the way we are." We can choose at any moment to follow through on our commitments, to live in integrity and wholeness.

You might be tempted to believe the limiting voice that says, "I'm just not wired to make and keep commitments," or, "It's too hard and not that big of a deal." Believing you're not capable is a racket, and the importance and power of commitment cannot be overstated. When we become people who vigilantly seek to keep (or renegotiate, in extreme cases) commitments, our lives begin to shift in ways we could never imagine—our influence broadens radically; our confidence in ourselves and our abilities to accomplish great things skyrocket; and our relationships deepen and strengthen. When we decide to be someone who people know they can count on, all areas of our lives expand—trustworthiness impacts every relationship and every endeavor.

Start by committing to follow through, no matter what, on small things. It could be punctuality to your next meeting. It could be going to the gym one time this week. It could be any small commitment that will help you begin to build back that trust in yourself. Then you can take that superhero power of commitment, begin to make bold declarations toward massive projects, and watch them come to pass right before your eyes. And it is possible—not just for some people, but for you.

14

Seriously?

"I'm always amazed that people
take what I say seriously.
I don't even take what I am seriously."
~DAVID BOWIE

One helpful way to incorporate playfulness into our lives is to choose not to take ourselves, or even our work, so seriously. Sure, work with all your heart and passion, but as soon as work becomes a very serious and important matter, we tend to lose the play aspect, which takes away the fun and creativity.

I find in my own life that when I take myself too seriously it stems from some fear lurking beneath the surface, some story that I'm telling myself: that if I'm not perfect or if this project doesn't work out, then all opportunity will be lost to me—that this is the last good opportunity that will be coming my way.

When I get into this mindset of scarcity, I have a tendency to hold too tightly onto the project or relationship and squeeze the life out of it. It's very difficult to risk, experiment, and be creative—the usual ingredients for success—when we're terrified of failing.

In this state of being we tend to be more rigid and less flexible. And as obstacles come our way, as they inevitably will, anger and irritation tend to flare up in place of curiosity, so possibilities are more difficult to imagine and we become more and more frustrated.

If you've ever been in a dating relationship in which the other person held the relationship too tightly, you know the outcome; the relationship is suffocated. The same thing is true of business relationships and creative projects.

Have an open-hand policy about the projects and relationships you're engaging in. Allow these pursuits to breathe and go in directions not originally anticipated. This comes in part from believing that the universe (or God or Karma) is conspiring to work in our favor (which is true) and that there is an abundance of opportunity (which there is) if you slow down long enough to see it. This doesn't mean that we only half-heartedly work toward relationships and goals, of course, but that we allow these projects and relationships a measure of freedom to come or go. This allows us to be more objective and neutral and therefore better-equipped to creatively contribute and imaginatively troubleshoot barriers as they arise.

Another way that taking ourselves too seriously interferes with our goals is through an unwavering drive to be right. This manifestation of taking ourselves too seriously generally comes from a fear of being out of control, or more appropriately, losing the perception of control. Being in complete control is an illusion but there is some part of us that strives for that safe feeling. The danger of the drives to be in control and to be right is that they are often in direct competition with the visions we've created for ourselves.

There are four main categories of desires that war against our visions and become roadblocks to success: *looking good* (reputation or outward appearance), *feeling good* (comfort or escape), *being right* (pride, judgment, resistance to being corrected), and *being in control* (needing to be safe and free from failure or emotional pain).

While taking ourselves too seriously predominantly falls into the latter two categories, an argument can be made for the relevance and application of any one of them. This is why taking ourselves too seriously is dangerous; there is an infinite number of pitfalls and places to get stuck.

One way we can break out of taking ourselves so damn seriously is to choose to be silly on occasion and laugh at ourselves when we mess up rather than indulging in shame and self-judgment. There is a playful goofball in every one of us, but most of us lose that side of ourselves somewhere along the way. This is unfortunate because that is the place where imagination, creativity, fun, and play reside, and it's through those attributes that great ideas, great wealth, and great relationships are fostered.

I recently saw the Disney Pixar animated film, *Inside Out*, which is a brilliant depiction of how our thoughts and inner voices dictate our feelings and actions. The scene that really struck me, and brought me to tears, was the one in which the main character Riley experienced some hardships, and there was a shift in her mindset. All of a sudden her life began to occur to her as very serious and very difficult as she entered her teen years and moved to a different part of the country with her family. We could visually see inside her head that all the memories of her being silly and playful were repressed in a moment, and "Goofball Island," where all of her fun, goofy experiences were created, collapsed onto itself and fell into the pit of lost and discarded thoughts and memories. It was a reminder of how easy it is to lose our senses of play at an early age and begin taking ourselves and our lives too seriously.

The good news is that we can reclaim that part of us; it's not dead and gone forever—just in hibernation until we reawaken it. One way I've been rehabilitating my own sense of play and systematically chipping away at the part of myself that takes my life far too seriously is by taking improv classes. Practicing improv has helped me get out of my head, into my body, and onto rediscovering the inner goofball that I had abandoned so many years ago.

There are many creative ways to reclaim this lost sense of fun and playfulness, which can be discovered simply by taking the initiative to create opportunities to not take ourselves seriously, laugh at ourselves, and make games out of the things that seem so dire.

Do you find that you sometimes take yourself, your life, and your job far too seriously? What are some ways that you could reclaim your inner goofball and add some levity to your life and the lives of those around you? It's usually the people around us that feel like they're serving out a prison sentence when we are in the habit of perpetually taking ourselves too seriously. Maybe your prescription is to watch a couple of comedies this week, or maybe it's to use a funny accent at the checkout counter in the grocery store; whatever you decide would be fun and playful. It's from this place of levity that possibility begins to open up in a new, fresh way.

15

Tell Someone

"As iron sharpens iron,
so one person sharpens another."
~Hebrew Proverb

A great way to leverage the power of discipline and momentum is to set up structures of accountability in our lives, because we do better when others are watching. This is a principle that uses the ego against itself to produce the results that we really want in life.

When I'm not really serious about going after something, even if I genuinely want it, then I won't write it down and I won't tell anybody about it, because I know that once I do there will be a certain level of accountability. And I don't want to feel the shame (although shame is always a choice) and embarrassment if I'm unable to accomplish the goal. And I certainly don't want to look like a failure in front of others.

This can become a hiding place, a stuck place, and a racket for me, if I let it. When I choose to stay stuck in this way it actually comes from a deep understanding of the power of this principle—that my ego will be at stake if I set up structures of accountability and fail to follow through. So, I always have the option of leveraging this principle in a way that fosters the accomplishment of my goals, or avoiding accountability in order to stay safely, anonymously unaccountable.

If it's true that we do better when others are aware of what we want and what we say we're after—and if we want to avoid the pain of looking like a failure in front of other people—then we can use this principle to be more successful in any endeavor we choose.

This principle is one of the reasons that the various twelve-step rehab programs are so effective. They understand the power of accountability on a one-on-one level, through their use of sponsors, a sense of community, and regular meetings—along with compassion, understanding, and support. These aspects of accountability to free people from addiction and can also be used to accomplish any number of additional goals we want to go after.

As I've mentioned, I avoided writing a book for a decade or so, but once I finally decided to write my first book, *The Voice of Your Dreams*, I began telling as many people as possible about it. And as people asked me what was going on in my life I began to talk about the book, what page I was on, and the (arbitrary, self-created) due date I had set for myself to complete the writing. I even let my wide network of followers on YouTube know the same. I did all this because I knew that I would be much more motivated day after day if a lot of people knew what I was up to. Since I know that two of my core desires are to look good in front of others and be seen as a person who follows through with commitments, this is a way to keep a fire lit under my butt and remain in action.

This idea of accountability works in tandem with making a declaration. Making declarations alone is a powerful way to begin shifting the future that we see coming toward us, and therefore the future that we begin to live into. And when we fuse that together with the power of accountability, we strengthen it even more.

I remember when I was just about to complete graduate school, I decided that I wanted to go to Europe for a few weeks to travel around and have an adventure before beginning my post graduate job. I didn't have much money, didn't know anybody in Europe, and didn't know how I was going to pull it off. But I was determined to go and began saying to people, "I'm going to Europe right after graduation." I didn't say that I was thinking about it or hoped to go but that I was going.

So, I was making a declaration (a form of commitment) and also beginning to build structures of accountability. As I continued to tell more and more people, all kinds of opportunities began to arise. One person said, "Did you know that you can use your .edu email address and get half off your plane ticket?" and another said, "Did you know James has an internship in Europe and is staying with the American Ambassador to London? You may be able to connect up with him," and another said, "Make sure you look into hostels. It's the most fun and inexpensive way to travel through Europe."

I continue to use this principle as a leverage point in my life. In fact, I just added into my weekly schedule a video call with two other executive coaches, in which we all take turns making declarations for what we're committed to for the week. This gives me an opportunity to not only tell someone what I'm up to as a declaration, but also to create a structure of accountability as an extra jolt of power and motivation to get things done.

I also have a trusted friend to whom I've made myself accountable for more than a decade in regards to being a good husband. We check in regularly concerning the things we've committed to as it relates to our relationships with our respective wives. We're committed to honoring our wives, and we believe that being disciplined and accountable is one of the primary ways to do that. We make our declarations about what we're committed to and also confess any areas that have not measured up to our stated commitments, much like someone would with a Catholic priest. There is an immense freedom that arises from coming clean with the deficit between what we've done and what we've said we're committed to. The truth really does have a way of setting us free. This is another potential benefit of setting up accountability structures: to help you be more successful relationally and more whole emotionally.

After graduation I did end up spending three weeks traveling all over London, Italy, and France. If you find yourself in Paris, make sure you stop by the Shakespeare and Company bookstore and pick up a copy of Hemingway's *A Moveable Feast*, and read it during your stay. You'll thank me later.

What have you been working on or wanting to get started on? Maybe it's time to do some traveling? Who can you tell? Take a moment to decide, and write it here or on a piece of paper.

16

Requests

*"Out of your vulnerabilities
will come your strength."*
~SIGMUND FREUD

During a coaching session a few years ago, I remember telling my coach that I was a tenacious person. He said, "Tenacious up until the point of making requests of others, right?"

You see, I sort of fancied myself a content loner. I thought that as long as I worked my butt off and pushed through fear that I would be good on my own, and that I didn't really need anybody else's help. Well, not only was this a very narcissistic, self-aggrandizing perspective, but it was also just flat out untrue—and it masked my colossal fear of rejection.

Human beings were built for community and thrive most around others. We're simply not wired for isolation, and we can't accomplish our destinies and overarching life goals without other people helping us succeed along the way. Whatever we can accomplish on our own is a vision much too small for us to even bother giving our time, energy, and focus pursuing. As Helen Keller says, "Alone we can do so little; together we can do so much."

We need one another if we want to grab hold of a dream that is bigger than we are. And there's nothing wrong with that. Most of us hate feeling like we need others because we associate it with weakness. Couple that with the growing cultural trend toward autonomy and narcissism, and we have the perfect storm of going it alone.

When we close ourselves off from others and choose isolation, we cut ourselves off from insights, connectedness, and accountability—all of which are great resources for reaching our dreams. While relationships can be messy and sometimes annoying, they are often the source of fresh perspectives and a way to get outside of our comfort zones, which is where all breakthroughs come from.

Also, it's more fun to win with others than it is to win alone. At least for me that has been the case. There is something more fulfilling about accomplishing goals and celebrating with the people who were a part of making them happen.

My big fear when it came to making requests of others was that people would say "no"—as if there's anything inherently bad about that. This fear came from the limiting voice in my head about what it would mean about me or my art if I experienced rejection. "They said 'no.' That must mean that I'm stupid, that I will never make anything of myself, and that my art sucks."

As I made requests regarding my film productions, I had a much different experience from what I had anticipated. To my surprise, I found that most people said "yes."

I also discovered that while I was avoiding making requests of others, thinking I was somehow shielding them from feeling obligated to do something they really didn't want to do, I was also boxing people out of my life. I was being selfish with my life and vision.

When I reached out and began making requests, many people decided to work with me because it was an opportunity to be in my life, not just part of the vision. I found that not only were they not put off by the request, but that they were also hungry for community and wanted to create something with like-minded people. So these requests, which also served as invitations into my life and vision, were taken by many as a gift.

Another related principle is to not say "no" for anybody. You see, for years I was saying "no" *for* people instead of actually allowing them to decide for themselves whether I had an opportunity in which they would like to take part.

The best example I have for this principle occurred during my senior year of college. I knew that I was going to go on and do graduate work, so I started accumulating and filling out applications for graduate schools. I had a handful in mind that I thought I'd be a good candidate for and had a decent chance of getting into. Then I had a couple of schools that I considered Hail Mary options: Princeton and Duke. In their divinity schools there were particular professors who I thought would be amazing to work under, programs that were a great fit for where I wanted to end up and what I wanted to study. But I hesitated to even apply to either school because I was already saying "no" for both of those schools—vehemently.

Part of the reason I felt insecure about applying was because I had applied to a summer program at another big name school, Notre Dame, and I wasn't accepted. So, I created a story about myself that I wasn't top school material—that I was able to work hard and get decent grades at a small school but would be laughed at by a "real" school.

Even though I was carrying that baggage along with me I decided to apply to both schools, mostly because I had a handful of professors who had graduated from both and repeatedly told me that I was a good fit. My thinking was that since the applications for those schools were due months before the others', I'd still have plenty of time to apply to my backup schools after getting "rejected" by Princeton and Duke.

It turns out that I got accepted to both and never had to apply to the schools that I was only moderately interested in attending. Imagine if I had said "no" for them, assuming that was the obvious answer.

Receiving a "yes" when a "no" is anticipated is great, but what happens when the answer is "no"—repeatedly?

Most people are terrified of the seemingly big, bad "NO!" but "no" only has as much power and meaning as we allow it to have. It is simply the verbalization that someone is not interested in your opportunity at this moment. And it's only when we choose to associate "no" with our deepest fears about how unworthy or untalented or unequipped we are that it becomes a crisis to us.

Then we start using words like "rejection." There really is no such thing as rejection. Now, we can feel reject-*ed*, but that's because we assign emotional weight to rejection where there really is none. Even though we might not be interested in that moment, our interests could change in the future. Both "yes" and "no" are neither bad nor good; they're just information. In fact, if you're not getting a "no" at all, then you're probably playing a small game in which you would benefit from increasing the stakes.

The final piece to this concept is that ambitious people ask for what they want. It's resourceful to speak up and ask for the things we want in life. We can stay stuck when we choose not to take advantage of making requests. When we begin to see the act of making requests as a way to invite people into our lives and grow in a way that allows us to be of better service to others, then our perceptions of making requests switch from the scarcity mindset of feeling like a beggar to the idea that we're contributing to those around

– 131 –

us. Each of us is a gift to others, and as long as we see our-selves as burdens or as completely self-sufficient, we block the joy of being a gift to another human being and allow-ing them the opportunity to be a gift to us.

So, what requests could you make today that would help you move closer to your dream? Who will you make requests of? The world is far more ready to say "yes" than we think it is. Are you willing to test it out? Take a minute now and write down five requests you would be willing to make—and to whom—that will move your dream forward.

17

Freedom Addict

"Seek freedom and become the captive of your desires.
Seek discipline and find your liberty."
~Frank Herbert

Freedom is a beautiful pursuit, but it doesn't come from the place that many think it does. It most often comes in the form of a word that tends to trigger a recoiling feeling in most people. I know it certainly used to for me. That word is *discipline*.

The principle is this: discipline equals freedom.

As a child I had this notion that freedom is doing whatever I want, whenever I want, regardless of how it may impact the lives of others. I wanted to be free from the tyranny of my parents' rules and the suffocation of my teachers' demands. If I could only be free to do as I pleased when I pleased, life would be good. I imagine it may have been similar for you.

The problem is that if we bring this same thinking into adolescence and adulthood, we discover quickly that the result of that philosophy is often addiction, broken relationships, and sometimes incarceration.

This concept of discipline equaling freedom first began to take shape in my life when I was around eleven or twelve years old and started playing guitar. I wanted to have the freedom and joy of simply being able to pick up the guitar and play songs—to play whatever I wanted and just swim in the music without a thought of what my hands were doing; just pure, otherworldly creation. But every time I picked up the guitar to play it sounded like, "pluck, pluck, strum, strum, pause, pause, strum."

It wasn't creation; it was tinkering.

Having a strong desire to sing and play guitar and to be a singer-songwriter, I began to lock myself away in my room for hours and hours at a time, practicing and learning songs that I loved. I noticed that there was a direct correlation between this discipline—doing the work regardless of whether I felt like it—and the free, joyful swimming in music that I wanted so badly.

Once I really got that discipline equals freedom, I began to change the way I related to discipline, to reframe what it meant to me. Over time I shifted my concept of discipline from this elusive beast that I couldn't quite tame to a useful helper that had seemingly magical powers. I began to understand it as an incredible leverage point, a powerful tool to help me attain freedom in all the different areas of my life.

The most obvious example of discipline's effect may be the discipline of regularly practicing vocal warm-ups and vocal exercises. It's clear that when we do this we acquire a freedom in the voice that didn't previously exist. Even now that I've been singing professionally for many years I still need to keep up with this discipline if I want continued freedom in my voice. If I don't keep up with my vocal routine, then my voice isn't as free to hit high notes, sing with ease, or resonate with the same power that is otherwise possible for me. Freedom as a singer comes from the discipline of regularly doing the work of building and strengthening the muscles in our vocal tracts.

The same is true, of course, for fitness. If we're disciplined and consistently go to the gym and eat right, we have the freedom of looking good, feeling good, having greater mental awareness, and having increased agility.

We can apply this to any area of life. When we get disciplined with our finances—by creating a budget, saving money, and choosing not to spend money we haven't already earned—we tend to get out of debt, create a financial buffer between ourselves and life's mishaps, and have the opportunities to invest rather than simply living from paycheck to paycheck. And even better than all that, we can create a degree of surplus in life that allows us to be more financially generous, because the most fun thing that we could ever do with money is to think of creative ways to give it away and enrich others' lives.

We intuitively know this principle to be true and have experienced its results, but mustering up this seemingly evasive discipline seems problematic for most people. We tell ourselves that there is some missing piece in our personalities or in our DNA or that we weren't taught it as kids so it's harder for us to summon it inside of ourselves.

But none of that is true.

What's generally missing is a clear vision of what it is that we really, really want. The more specific and real we make that vision, the more likely we are to get after it and make use of discipline more quickly.

The beginning of discipline is making a decision that we're going to take action—and then choosing the smallest task associated with the goal and getting busy working on it. Discipline is most often simply choosing to start again today what we committed to the day before.

Once we get into action, inspiration and desire show up. But when we wait until we eventually feel like doing something or for whenever inspiration strikes, we're usually waiting a long time—maybe a lifetime. But once we simply choose to get into action, the feelings, inspiration, excitement, and discipline nearly always follow.

Are you willing to alter your relationship to discipline, to give up the lie that somehow you're not a disciplined person and don't have what it takes to access it? We all have the same ability to access discipline and the glorious results it produces. Some of us simply have more practice than others. But no matter where you are on the continuum right now, you can build it by choosing to spend four minutes doing the thing that you're avoiding, the thing that could begin to create momentum in the project that you know would lead to the kind of future that you want to live into. If not four minutes, taking even just two minutes could help—anything to get the ball rolling.

Remember, the mind makes even the smallest tasks seem impossible when we try to picture what accomplishing them might take, but when we ignore that and simply choose to get into action, then we see that everything is much easier than it seemed. It takes less effort to get excited and inspired when we simply do the next small thing that will lead us toward the beautiful futures we're creating.

If we want freedom in the different areas of our lives, it doesn't come from seeking freedom; it comes as a result of discipline.

18

The Momentum Fulcrum

"Success requires first expending ten
units of effort to produce one unit of results.
Your momentum will then produce ten
units of results with each unit of effort."
~Charles J. Givens

Discipline can be a trusted friend in the pursuit of the results that we want in our lives. This may not be a revelatory piece of information, but what tends to be overlooked—in those times when we avoid discipline at all costs—is that discipline isn't the constant grind that we often perceive it to be. As we choose to apply discipline to a project, somewhere along the line that same discipline begins to morph into something else, something that feels effortless. And that something is momentum.

Momentum, like a superhero rushing to our aid, comes down and helps us go further, faster, and more effortlessly. As Charles J. Givens says, momentum allows us to produce ten times more with only ten percent of the originally exerted effort.

There is no doubt that at the very beginning of an endeavor there are often tasks that you don't necessarily want to do in order to get the project moving. But without taking the time to do them, we can never experience the glorious benefits of momentum.

There is a huge part of me that loves the idea of generating income and progress without the one-to-one ratio of time to output. That always felt so limiting to me. This is one of the reasons I became an entrepreneur in the first place—passive income. I wanted to continue to serve the world and make money while I'm sleeping, while on vacation, while I'm on a date-night with my wife, or while I'm creating another product or service that I love and know will positively impact humanity.

I remember that when I first began creating my online singing program, Superior Singing Method, I was putting nearly thirty hours a week into building the method, while working a couple other jobs. This went on day after day, month after month, and I wasn't even sure yet whether it would actually ever make any money or serve anybody. I believed it would, but I didn't know for sure.

All that time spent working on the site was building a momentum that I couldn't really measure but would serve me a hundredfold in the future. Today the site turns a good profit, and I work about thirty minutes a week to maintain it, sometimes more but often even less. Momentum shifted, and it takes much less effort to continue to grow the business.

The same principle applies to my voice. When I'm on top of my game and doing my vocal exercises regularly for a period of time, the momentum allows me to be performance-ready after a much shorter period of warm up.

And the same is true for the long-term game of singing. If I'm consistent with doing the work of practicing my singing and singing on a regular basis, and then I slack off for a few weeks or months even, it takes far less time to get my voice back into shape than if I had not laid the groundwork in the beginning.

In some ways this principle of momentum may be a discouragement to you. You may be thinking, "Well, that's all fine and good, but momentum takes a long time to establish, and I don't know if I have the willpower, or even desire, to be disciplined long enough for momentum to kick in." I often find myself in this boat until I remember that momentum has a short-term and long-term payoff, meaning that little spurts of momentum and the accompanying results show up even after just one or two short stints of action. If I go to the gym and workout even for one day I feel much better physically and mentally. That result and the new state of being give me the push I need to choose to continue for one more day, and that day gives me what it takes for the next day, and the next, and the next. Before

I know it, I've created a routine that has lasted months and has not only produced tremendous results, but has also built up all kinds of momentum that will continue to pay dividends for a long time.

Momentum creates tremendous power. It can multiply our efforts ten-, twenty-, or even a hundredfold, but only after we begin, that is, only after we commit to moving forward into action. After a while you won't know if you're producing the momentum or if it's simply carrying you.

Once one of my projects has gained a lot of momentum, I feel like the project is a wave that I'm surfing, and while I'm navigating my movements, it's the momentum that is driving the project forward. It takes little effort to continue to propel it. This is a beautiful and freeing feeling, and it all begins with a decision, a declaration, and the first few minutes of action.

Are you willing to play a game called "momentum" today? Here's how it works. You choose the thing for which you would like to produce momentum and then commit to working on it at least three days this week—five or six days being the ultimate goal. In this game, you pretend you're a robot and that feelings don't get a say in the matter. You're going to do this thing purely as an experiment and do it no matter what it takes. At the end of the week you'll check in with the results and how this activity is *occurring* to you, that is, whether you now feel like this whole endeavor is more possible and even more fun. Check in on your motivation and see if it's not much higher than it was before, now that you are actually seeing results and a greater degree of possibility.

Are you willing to take one minute right now and write that thing down, tell someone what you intend to do, and tell them to ask you about it later?

The fulcrum of momentum is a power that we all have access to but few really take advantage of. Are you willing to be one of the few?

19

The Habit

*"Successful people are simply those
with successful habits."*
~Brian Tracy

In American philosopher and psychologist William
James' famous work, *Principles of Psychology*, he says that
human beings are bundles of habits and that these habits
are important to our survival because they allow the brain
to partially shut off while performing everyday tasks that
would be nearly impossible to give attention to all at once
without wearing the brain out.

Habits serve to free up the mind from consciously
thinking, "Okay, it's time to get out of bed, so engage left
and right thigh muscles and abdomen muscles, lifting the
lower half of the body, and then simultaneously engage
each muscle of the right arm and swing toward the edge of
the bed, flexing and sliding the gluteal muscles and gently

placing feet on the ground. Bend forward and reach for pants, but make sure not to hit your head on the bed canopy support."

Certain actions are simply automatic, resulting from an established habit. And since we don't have to consciously think about each movement, we aren't bogged down with too much information overloading the bandwidths of our brains.

This is true for more complex habits like making breakfast in the morning—especially if you, like me, make the same thing every morning—and also like driving a car. While there are certain factors in our routines that may change and take more conscious thought, like when you're out of eggs and have to improvise or when you pull over to the side of the road for an ambulance on your way to work, a high percentage of our routines are automated.

Taking their cue from William James, scientists now say that habits emerge because the brain is constantly looking for ways to conserve effort, and that the brain stores habits in the basal ganglia section of the brain, which takes over at the onset of a habit, allowing the rest of the brain to sleep.

This automated system of the basal ganglia has its advantages and disadvantages. Some habits serve us on our journeys toward what we want in life, and others work against us. So, if it's true that successful people are simply those who have successful habits, it would be worth looking into how to create new, resourceful habits and transform others that are not in line with our visions for our lives.

In Pulitzer Prize winning reporter Charles Duhigg's book, *The Power of Habit*, he says that forming and transforming habits is much easier when we understand the anatomy of a habit, that is, how a habit forms and sticks. He breaks it down into three main components: the *cue*, the *routine*, and the *reward*. He calls this the "habit loop."

As an example, let's take the everyday occurrence of receiving a text message or email on your phone. The *cue* is the familiar chime the phone makes when a new text or email comes in. The *routine*, for most of us, is to immediately look at the phone to see who it is and what they've said. And the *reward* may vary from person to person, but is likely somewhere along the lines of feeling connected, feeling in the know, or feeling important.

Another example from my life is my vocal warm up and warm down exercises. I primarily do these in my car, since it's a place where I'm often alone and in an enclosed space where I won't be bothering anyone. For many years, when CDs were more common, I would get into my car and see my vocal exercise CD on the shelf just below the CD player; this was my cue. Then, after having seen the CD and having been reminded that I hadn't yet done my vocal exercises for the day, I'd pop the CD in the player and do my vocal scales while driving to my destination; that was my routine. After finishing my vocal routine I would feel good about myself for having done something that is going to move my dream of being a great singer forward, and I would feel the greater sense of freedom in my voice as I sang along to the radio; that was my reward.

That is how a habit is created. And most of us know which habits would benefit us the most, but often get stuck on the idea that we don't have enough discipline or willpower to start a practice that would serve us (and ultimately the world, in most cases) powerfully.

It begins with a choice—a commitment to start the practice. From there we get very clear about what the cues and rewards are and set the habit in motion. We have a lot of habits that we establish without full consciousness, that is, without realizing that we're forming a habit—like watching television every night after dinner or smoking a few cigarettes with friends as a kid—but we can also leverage this formula to intentionally create the habits in our lives that will help us reach our dreams, goals, and most heroic selves.

While my vocal exercise habit in the car was beneficial, I didn't form it intentionally; it just sort of happened. On the other hand, one habit that I purposefully formed using the habit loop formula is my morning workout.

When I thought about forming this habit, I started the formula backwards; I first considered the reward of habitually exercising. It may be fairly obvious what the benefits of working out are, but I had to get a clearer vision of which rewards truly motivated me. I wanted to be healthy and alive, not bogged down by a sluggish body. I wanted to be sharp mentally, so that I could excel at coaching and making decisions throughout the day.

Exercise also helped me to feel better emotionally, from the validation of making a decision to work out and following through on it and also from the endorphins that are naturally released during exercise. All of these benefits connected with me, but not necessarily enough for me to push through and exercise everyday.

It turns out that one of my biggest motivators was looking good. In my mind I associated being a performer with being in good shape, so working out became one way to indirectly pursue my dream. Realizing what really motivated me meant that I could leverage my ego in order to produce a habit that sticks, that is, to actually get myself to do what I knew was in my best interest for all the reasons stated above.

The secret to the principle of forming any habit is discovering the reward that connects the most with you. Once you choose a reward that motivates you, you make sure to allow yourself to enjoy the reward each time. Allow yourself to eat some dark chocolate after your workout or enjoy a guilt-free movie night at the end of the first week of faithfully exercising. Do whatever you can to get your habit started.

So after I got really clear about my rewards, I decided to deliberately set my "cue," running shoes, in plain sight as soon as I woke up. So, the first thing I do when I get out of bed is see my running shoes and workout clothes next to the bed, and I put them on. This gets me out the door, and when I'm at the gym I follow one of my two preset workouts; all of this, of course, is the routine. After I'm done working out I experience all my rewards.

Okay, but what about habits that we don't want—the ones that are annoying, destructive, or just not resourceful? How can we transform those? Understanding the habit loop is the way we create new habits, and it's also the way to alter current habits. Since habits are most often (if not always) transformed, not eradicated, we can use the "cue, routine, and reward" formula to turn old habits into new ones—ones that are more resourceful. The key here is also discovering what reward we're seeking, or to put it differently, what desire we're fulfilling. Once we discover what we're craving, that is, the reward, we can change the routine, while keeping the same cue and reward.

For example, author and behavioral psychology pioneer Nathan Azrin ran a successful study in which he was able to quickly reverse clients' nail biting habits and other nervous tics without attempting to eradicate the habits themselves but by targeting the routine. In his habit-reversal method he had the client describe the cravings and determine what the cue was. Once the client was aware of what was driving her to continue biting her nails and what the specific cue was, she could insert a different activity as a replacement.

Every time the client would notice the cue Azrin would have her put her arms down by her sides and clench her fists until she felt tension in her hands and arms. If this new routine behavior interfered with her daily activities, he would have her grab and squeeze an object nearby until she felt a degree of tension in her hands and arms. This new routine would deliver the same reward of physical stimulation.

Another important aspect of the habit-eliminating puzzle is that if we're not all-in for changing the habit, then change is not likely to take place. Self-discipline is necessary to alter a routine, and that discipline is the most potent when we crank the want-to up to a critical mass.

This *way of being*, having a committed interest in replacing or creating a habit, is one of the most important pieces of the puzzle, since without it, there is rarely ever success. And this is true for any endeavor in life. A casual interest in becoming a great singer is not enough to set the habits that create success in motion. There needs to be a strong desire that produces a certain degree of grit and tenacity.

Another important aspect of creating or replacing a habit is belief—belief that it's not only possible to replace a habit but also that it's possible for *you* to transform the habit that isn't serving you. And this belief usually comes in the form of some type of community—certainly it could be in a larger community like a church or a club, but it could also be a community of two people. I've seen my one-on-one clients change habits radically just within the community of the two of us. One of my clients, who said to me, "I'm not a reader," has read twenty one books in the five months or so that we've been coaching—about one book per week. I would say she's altered her habits so much that any onlooker would confidently say that she is most definitely a reader.

Alcoholics Anonymous uses community and belief as a foundation of transforming the habit known as an addiction. There is a commitment within the AA community to attend regular meetings and to believe not only that it's possible to change the habit of drinking but also that there is a Higher Power aiding them along the way.

One of the foundational limiting voices says, "I'm not going to be able to do this." This is a racket with lots of payoffs, which is why believing in your ability to change is such an important ingredient in reforming a habit and also in accomplishing your goals in life. If we don't believe it's possible for us, we won't even try; after all, "What's the point? Why waste my time on something that's never going to happen?"

William James found himself in this position early in his life. Having contemplated suicide for months on end as a young adult, he chose to believe for one year that change is possible, that free will did exist, and that habits could be altered. He didn't know if these things were true but *chose* to believe it for a year to see what might happen. He chose to change his habits, but more importantly his way of *being*, and thus what he believed was possible for him and the world around him.

Belief isn't something you have or don't have, as most people think; it is a choice. We have a choice to believe something is true about ourselves and the world around us, begin to act as if it is true, and watch as our lives begin to transform. This doesn't mean that we never waver in our beliefs, but when we do we have the choice to get back on track and start seeing the evidence and results of that belief.

One of my professors used to tell a story about a young priest who came to one of his elders because he was struggling with his faith. His elder said to him, "Recite the Apostles Creed." The young priest said, "But I don't believe in what it says." The Elder repeated, "Recite the Apostles Creed." The young priest said again, "But you don't understand. I don't believe it." The Elder said again, "Recite the Apostles Creed."

We form beliefs by first choosing to do so, and we make our beliefs firm through repetition and immersion in a community of like-minded people, just like the attendees of the AA meetings do.

William James' life changed radically, and he became one of the most influential American-born philosophers and thinkers of the late nineteenth century. And because of his innovative contributions to the field of psychology he was labeled the "Father of American Psychology." His choice to believe that he could alter his life and his habits allowed him to look for, and recognize, the evidence of this change and continue to build a case for the possibility of change through repetition.

Habits are not destiny. We have the power to form and reform any habit we choose. All habits are malleable. This is good news, since successful people are simply those with successful habits.

The easiest way to do this is to have a plan. A habit begins with a choice and when the prescribed routine is practiced enough we stop thinking about it. The brain kicks into automatic mode and continues to follow the map, like water flowing downhill into the ravine it has cut out for itself. Since this automatic behavior kicks in on its own, we alter the habit by going back to the place where it started, that is, the place where it initially formed. We need to override automatic habits with conscious choice.

Which habits would you like to form in your life? Are you willing to think through and experiment with potential rewards, cues, and routines? Are you willing to write down at least one right now? Which habits would you like to change? Yes, the one you're thinking of right now. Are you willing to seek out the reward you're craving, construct a cue for the behavior, and repeat a different routine until it becomes automatic? Imagine how free you would feel if you were released from the habit that you know isn't leading you to your most heroic and fulfilling life. Think about how others may experience a greater sense of freedom in themselves or in you if this habit were transformed. Are you willing to start now?

PART V

HEALTHY LIVING

20

The Un-Had Conversation

*"I learned that a long walk
and calm conversation are an incredible combination
if you want to build a bridge."*
~Seth Godin

I remember sitting down with a potential coaching client in a restaurant, and after a couple minutes, I said, "I find that the un-had conversations in our lives have a tendency to run our lives." He immediately burst into tears. He had been holding in the pressure of an un-had conversation with his ex-girlfriend for over a year, and the very idea of breaking the silence and having that conversation with her caused his emotions to pour out in the middle of a crowded hipster joint in the NoHo Arts District of Los Angeles.

The things we avoid hold the reins in our lives, and many of the things we avoid boil down to a conversation that needs to be had that we haven't yet initiated. When we are holding onto an un-had conversation, it begins to take up space in our minds—bandwidth that could otherwise be used to create the future we want to live into. It drains our energy and clouds our focus, and we begin to feel like we're overwhelmed with life's daily circumstances, when really, it's all the thoughts about the un-had conversations in our minds that we're holding onto—and semi-consciously rehearsing—that are taking up the better part of our brains' creative capacity. It's no wonder we feel overwhelmed so easily when unanticipated circumstances arise.

A friend or family member may pop into our minds, and we try to dismiss the thought quickly or begin thinking about what we ought to do, with thoughts like, "Ah, I really should call her and tell her how I feel." We may begin to forecast how the conversation might go and remember how hard-headed we perceive the person to have been in the past so, again, we attempt to stuff the thought back down, since, "It's not going to do any good to bring it up now," we tell ourselves, or, "I can't handle these emotions with all I've got going on at the moment."

This can work for a time, but it will usually rear it's ugly head again soon, and so we continue the pattern of resisting the thought, which, as we know, gives it more weight—since what we resist persists—and therefore takes up more bandwidth, leaving us feeling a general gnawing sense of stress and discontentment.

Just recently I found myself nursing an un-had conversation with a long-time friend of mine with whom I co-produced a film. We had had some disagreements about some of the content of the film. He was upset, feeling like the film was turning into something different than what he had originally wanted. We had worked on the film, on and off, for nearly two years, and had many discussions about his grievances, but there was still a measure of tension between us—an un-had conversation that went deeper than these previous conversations had gone.

I found that I would get agitated whenever I thought about him or about the film. I had this feeling that things weren't completely resolved. I wanted to be free from this tension and free up some more bandwidth in my mind, so I decided to get a clear agreement with him. I asked him what it would take to have him feel like he was honored—as far as the project was concerned—and if I were to accommodate that, could we put this behind us for good and move forward. We came to an agreement, and I immediately felt a huge weight lift off my shoulders.

What un-had conversations are weighing on you right now? Often there is a main one that is eating you up inside. Are you willing to reach out to that person this week, today even, and initiate the conversation that can lead you toward a greater sense of freedom in your life?

Initiating that conversation can be the beginning of building that bridge toward a healthier relationship. And it could also eliminate some of that white noise in your mind to free up some room for creative thoughts that will lead you toward the life that you really want. Our unending pursuit is to have a clear mind by clearing out all un-had conversations. This leads to a life of peace, which means far greater—and more creatively driven—productivity.

21

He Doesn't Deserve It

"When you forgive,
you in no way change the past—
but you sure do change the future."
~Bernard Meltzer

Un-had conversations are often times the result of some
level of resentment and a lack of forgiveness. I end up
talking a lot about the power of forgiveness in my coaching sessions because the tendency to be unforgiving is a
common and powerful stuck place that puts the brakes on
progress—on attaining the things we really want in life.
Success is rarely possible in life when we choose not to
forgive.

Now, that doesn't mean that some people who harbor
deep resentments can't accomplish a lot (there is a certain
amount of bulldozing drive that comes from anger and
the desire to prove something); just that those achievements will often seem more like a mouthful of ash if the

bitterness of not forgiving hasn't been uprooted. It's difficult to enjoy any sort of success and accomplishment when peace is absent.

More often than not—in my experience and the experience of my clients—being unforgiving and its associated bitterness carve out a path for us that doesn't lead to success or the fulfillment of our dreams because it is a powerless, victimized position that keeps us tied to our pasts. It's very difficult to take new ground when we choose to live in the past. This is true whether we fail to forgive ourselves, which shows up as shame, or if we fail to forgive someone or something else, which shows up as judgment.

When we dig in our heels and get into a fixed position (feeling stubbornly resolved about someone or something), we remain stuck where we are, unable to move forward. It's as if part of us has been frozen in amber.

The judgment enters the picture when we see the offender as being fixed in a certain behavior or fixed as an unchanging or unchangeable person, thinking, "This is who they are, how they are, and how they will always be." As long as we see them as unchanging, we remain unchanged in our thoughts and actions toward them, stuck in a cycle of the same "unwanted" results in our own lives. This shuts down opportunity and new possibility in the present moment and therefore the future, because nothing new can be accomplished without new beliefs, thoughts, and actions.

Forgiveness is a way to break out of this pattern.

Forgiveness comes in the form of giving up one's pride, stubborn resolve, and fixed opinions regarding any given person or situation. The comfort of feeling like you're the one who's right is one of the major payoffs from the racket of not forgiving.

Choosing not to forgive is a racket because it is a choice to continue being victimized by a past hurt. Now, that doesn't mean that our past hurts and offenses are not valid or that we weren't legitimately victimized. It just means that while we may have *been* victims, we have the choice whether to continue to *be* victimized by the pain.

There are some seemingly short-term payoffs of choosing not to forgive and living as a victim, as is true for all rackets. As long as he is the *offender*, we get to live as the *offended*. As long as she treated us wrongfully, we get to be right about how wrong she is.

There is a certain safety in the offended state, that is, the safe victimized position where we feel like our destructive behaviors are justified and the responsibility is quickly blamed on the other, who is, after all, the offender. But this is a stuck place that isn't resourceful in terms of creating and attaining the lives that we really want, because it's difficult to be creative and optimistic and see possibility when we're spending so much of our bandwidths nursing and rehearsing our past hurts and offenses.

Sometimes *we* are the offenders. Sometimes the one falling short on commitments, priorities, and relationships is the person in the mirror. When this is the case, and we refuse to forgive ourselves, we experience shame.

Living in shame was a way of existence for me for the better part of my life. Don't get me wrong; jumping into shame is still a strong temptation. One bit of shame that I only recently let go of is the fact that I was engaged to be married about a decade before proposing to the woman to whom I am now married. This first engagement was to a woman I'll call "Julie." Back then I came to a realization, through some good mentoring, that Julie and I were not a good fit, so I called off the engagement a couple months before our wedding day. Even though Julie sent me a letter a couple years after the broken engagement saying that she forgave me, I felt as though I couldn't let myself off the hook.

I was so ashamed of this for so long that it began to eat me up inside. Whenever I was dating another woman I would be terrified to tell her this "dark secret" for fear that she would run, that she would think that I wouldn't ever follow through and commit relationally. It wasn't until I saw shame for what it actually is that I was able to begin the process of letting it go.

Shame is the emotional baggage of guilt and is an emergency brake on taking new ground. It's what's telling us, "You can't get there," and, "You're not worthy," based on broken promises that we have made to ourselves or others in the past. We no longer trust ourselves or our abilities to change, so instead of forgiving ourselves, we resolve that we don't deserve peace and choose shame as an alternative.

Shame is a self-protective process, not a spiritual one. It's often misconstrued as a spiritual way to lead us to some type of reconciliation with oneself or perhaps God or the universe. But shame doesn't lead to reconciliation; it leads to isolation because there is safety there. In isolation, we are the only ones in the audience condemning ourselves, free from the judgmental finger-pointing of others. It is a way of grasping onto control, because we can avoid the consequences of our actions for as long as we continue to hide. Shame is an isolation strategy that keeps us in the past.

Avoid shame; it binds us to destructive patterns of the past, which lends toward carrying them into the future—only to bring about the same unwanted results over and over again.

When we forgive ourselves and forgive others we gain our power, energy, and vitality back. Forgiveness puts an end to the constant drain of giving our power away to the person or institution we choose not to forgive.

The process of forgiving can be elusive for many. I often hear my clients say, "I tried to forgive her, but it didn't take." Another common response is, "Yeah, I already forgave him," but when I press further, I discover that my client would still like to choke the guy out, given the opportunity. Forgiveness didn't take in this instance either.

One principle of forgiveness is that it is both an event and a process. When I hear statements like the ones above, it usually means that the event happened, but the process part was neglected.

Let's first talk about the event. There is a specific time and place where we decide to forgive somebody. There is a declaration of pardon, meaning that this individual or institution no longer owes us anything.

Getting very specific about what the offender *owes* us is an important step in the event part of forgiveness so that those particular offenses can be let go—maybe it's fifty dollars, maybe it's more respect, maybe it's a new childhood. Listing the offenses and writing them down helps us to get some distance from them. It's no longer a parasite of the mind eating away at our joy and well-being. It now becomes more clear what we're actually grieving, and it allows us to get out of the nebulous cycle of gnawing, nameless pain. Once we have language for it and see it on the piece of paper, it becomes more finite and manageable. Not only that, but the more specific the pardon, the more efficacious the forgiveness. A blanket statement of forgiveness doesn't have the same freeing power as a very precise acquittal.

Doing this once—the *event* part—doesn't always do the trick. This is where the *process* comes into the picture.

Forgiveness is a decision we make every day. Just like love, it's not a feeling or a one-time declaration. Both love and forgiveness become deeper and more firmly rooted over time as we stay committed to them and build momentum in their direction.

Love is not only analogous to forgiveness; it is also the antidote to the disease of refusing to forgive. One of the primary reasons we don't forgive is fear, which comes from mistrust and a deep desire to avoid more pain, and since perfect love drives out fear, love is the route back home to a centered peace in relationships. In this realm of peace, resentments and rightness are given up and life pours back in, cultivating a love for ourselves and for the humanity of the offender.

One way we could love the offender, which may sound like the very last thing you're interested in right now (remember, this is about freeing ourselves from the hold of this racket), is to begin to pray or wish good things for them. This may be a tough sell, but it's an effective way to begin to remember the humanity we have in common with the offender and more quickly melt the bitterness away from our hearts. This part of the process allows us to, at least momentarily, let go of the strong case we've built against them, the case that gives us permission to continue to hold onto the grudge and receive the payoffs for doing so.

The amount of time this process takes depends on how deep the pain is, and more importantly, how long we've been benefiting from the pain—the value in being a victim.

As an aside, I'm sure that seems incredibly insensitive, and I don't want to overlook the pain that feels very real and often very deep, but my purpose here is to give practical tools on how to experience freedom: a freedom that will lead to a fuller, freer life and ultimately to a bigger future, one worth living toward.

Consider the payoffs that we might choose by refusing to forgive and remaining victimized. We've mentioned a few here already. We get to deny ownership and responsibility. We get to refuse discovery of how we may have played a role in the outcome of the offense (as an aside, in the case of a child, and particularly when abuse is a factor, the child has no responsibility to take ownership of the offense itself). We get to (potentially) not trust men or not trust women, which allows us to play it safe in relationships. We get to feel right and feel the perceived power of anger, resentment, and self-righteousness.

The quicker we can give up these temporary payoffs, the sooner we can alleviate our resentments. The process of forgiveness is a decision that is more effective as it is renewed...until it no longer has a hold on us.

Grief is another important step in the process of forgiving, and is a process in itself. There is a liberating power in grieving even the smallest of disappointments and offenses. This allows the heart to feel a degree of closure and release the pain of disillusionment, regret, and sadness.

We can grieve not only what was lost in the offense but also the continued pain we create for ourselves while we refuse to forgive and hold onto being right, staying a victim long after the victimization occurred.

Another common element in the refusal to forgive comes through in statements like, "I'm not forgiving him. He doesn't *deserve* it." There's a certain part of us that feels like we're hurting the offender by ignoring her, by icing her out, and by not forgiving. In some way, it feels like a form of retribution.

When we choose not to forgive someone, often times they are none the wiser. They are going about their lives—half the time not even aware that they offended us—completely unscathed and unaware that we are being eaten up inside by resentment and anger. It's like what Anne Lamott says in her book, *Traveling Mercies*, "Not forgiving is like drinking rat poison and waiting for the rat to die." Forgiveness isn't about doing a favor for the *offender* but about granting freedom to yourself, the *offended*.

Lack of forgiveness is a bitterness that takes root in our hearts and begins to choke the life out of us. It's a poison that slowly kills our joy and our perspectives and makes loving ourselves and others more and more difficult. The question isn't whether the offender deserves our forgiveness; it's whether we want to be free from the debilitating effects of the rat poison.

Another place that some people get stuck is thinking that they need to approach the offender and confront them about their grievances in order for forgiveness to take place. Sometimes this is the right course of action, while other times it's better to do the work of forgiveness alone.

Forgiveness is between you and yourself. Forgiveness is not about the other person. Your job is to take care of you. You are one hundred percent responsible for fifty percent of all your relationships, and that fifty percent is you. It may be resourceful to go and talk with the other person, but the work of forgiveness can be done within your own heart, since that's where the resentment exists.

I had one client who had some serious grievances with her father, who had died nearly a decade before we started coaching together. She was stuck around the idea of forgiveness because she felt as though she had lost her window to speak with him. I suggested that she write a letter, addressed to her deceased father, and let him know about how she felt and all that she has now chosen to forgive. She did so and found it to be a healing exercise that afforded her a deeper sense of freedom from her thoughts and memories of her father.

Failing to forgive is a stuck place that undermines our potential; it shuts down opportunities and causes us to live with the foggy white noise of resentment constantly brewing in the background of our minds and thoughts.

It can sneak up on us, too. It's not always what we perceive to be a deep, obvious wound from childhood or from a divorce or betrayal. We can unconsciously allow small disappointments in everyday life to lodge into our hearts. These are the disappointments that we don't realize are there until we stop and take an inventory of how we're feeling and what thoughts and interpretations we're nursing that are making us so angry or constantly dissatisfied with life.

Who might you be holding out on forgiving? It's usually pretty easy to discover. Who would you like to punch right now? Who have you been quietly punitive toward recently? Who would you secretly (or not so secretly) like to see fail? Are you willing to transform that un-had conversation into a *had* conversation?

Are you willing to do the work of forgiveness in your own heart, for the sake of your future and all the people you interact with daily, and free yourself, even if you're not interested in talking to the person directly or reconciling the relationship itself? Would you be willing to give up being right in order to be free, in order to be at peace and to have a future worth living into where beauty and life rush back into you?

There is another option; there is another choice; there is another chance for a new future—forgiveness will not change the past but it sure as hell can radically change your future.

22

I Apologize

"Forgiveness says you are given another chance
to make a new beginning."
~DESMOND TUTU

Another important piece of honoring your word is that integrity isn't about being perfect all the time. Honoring your word is not about simply never breaking your promises. Certainly that is the goal, but all is not lost when it happens. Trust with another person can be restored after you've broken a promise with them.

However, restoring the relationship and trust will require a full ownership of the fractured connection with the other person. This is usually best done with a certain amount of humility, such as asking the other person to forgive you for the offense. I use the word "forgive" deliberately here as a distinction from saying "sorry" or especially "I apologize."

You see, when we break a commitment to someone else they often feel like they've been robbed of their power, since someone has taken advantage of the trust that they willfully extended—or at least it feels this way to the offended party. So a simple "sorry" can pacify the situation but will rarely restore trust in the relationship because you still haven't necessarily taken full ownership of the wrong.

An "apology" is actually a defense of or a justification for something, a vindicating speech against an accusation. As long as we are in the position of defending or justifying our broken commitments, we aren't taking ownership of them. Taking ownership of a broken commitment is how trust is restored, and thus apologies stand in direct contrast to restoring trust.

This is why asking for forgiveness can be so difficult to do. It places the power of choice back into the hands of the offended party. While "sorry" doesn't need a response, since it holds onto the control of the situation, asking for forgiveness carries with it an admission of guilt and ownership of the offense. This request for forgiveness passes the control back over to the other person, validating their importance and allowing them to choose whether to pardon you. This act has a way of restoring the offended person's confidence in the offender and clearing up the relationship in a more complete way.

On the one hand, this can seem like mere semantics—just using another word for the same thing. But as I've applied this principle in my life, I've noticed a shift in my relationships and in others' confidence in me as a man of my word.

As I began to do this, I noticed that others would feel slightly uncomfortable at first, since it's become such an uncommon practice. But I've also noticed that they feel honored and vindicated in a way that allows them to let go of their resentments that were beginning to grow, as if the wrong has been wiped away.

This practice also has another practical advantage. It allows us to own our choices, whereas not owning the outcomes of our choices puts us into the victim mindset and strips us of our own rightful power.

Seeking forgiveness gives us a much better opportunity to have a brand new beginning, free of resentment and mistrust from the offended party.

Can you think of someone right now whom you could ask forgiveness of and, subsequently, create a better relationship with? Are you willing to commit to doing that today?

23

Thanks, Man

*"Gratitude is the healthiest of all human emotions.
The more you express gratitude for what you have,
the more likely you will have even more
to express gratitude for."*
~ZIG ZIGLAR

Gratitude is a habit; it's a routine that is practiced.

Living a life of gratitude doesn't come from having more to be grateful for—more money, more opportunity, more success, and so on—but rather, from slowing down long enough to recognize and give thanks for the abundance that already exists in our lives.

Now, this isn't a revelatory idea, of course. I'm certain you've heard this in some form from your parents or have seen it on a refrigerator magnet or on a small wooden sign hanging by a wire in someone's bathroom. But the real secret is how our *being*—how we present ourselves in life and in conversation with others—changes when we choose to practice gratitude. There is also a measure of joy that comes as a result of this discipline—not to mention the ability to quickly establish great relationships with others.

Being appreciative pulls us out of a scarcity mindset and reminds us how much good exists in our lives. It draws us into contentment and peace more than just about any other practice. Gratitude fosters an optimistic mindset that opens up new opportunities and possibilities for us.

One practice that has become a great resource for me is a list in the notes section of my phone called "I'm Thankful For." It's a list that I add to on a regular basis and rehearse several days a week. I look over the list most mornings, and it has a way of refocusing me onto what is real and true in my life; that is, what my blessings are. It's so easy to begin the day with complaints about pain or workload or bad weather, but this creates a space where I can work on the optimistic muscle and get all of its benefits first thing in the morning to set the stage for how the rest of my day will go. If I lose focus, and my sense of entitlement begins to rise up again, I can always pause and take a look at my list or simply ask myself the question, "What is there in this particular situation that I am grateful for?"

This question is a great way to practice appreciating people. We have an opportunity everyday and in every situation in which we interact with others, whether it's with a co-worker, spouse, doctor, or barrister, to consciously think about what we appreciate about that person and then tell them. We can be specific about what we appreciate, saying, for example, "Hi there. I wanted to tell you that the last time I was here you were very kind to me and helped me work out my paperwork, and I really appreciated that."

Rather than allowing the opportunity to pass, we can use gratitude to build that person up, re-focus our own ways of being, and enhance the interpersonal relationship. This becomes a practice—a habit. It's not that some people are just nice and appreciative because of a particular personality type. Those who are appreciative on a regular basis have created a habit of gratitude that has become of a way of being—something that now appears to be a personality trait. This is true for everyone who is regularly appreciative, and can be true for you too.

Gratitude is like a muscle that we have the choice to work and grow. There is a power of appreciation in us that lies dormant until we get into the gratefulness gym and work it out. In the case of appreciation, it is strengthened with use. The more we practice it with the people in our day-to-day lives, the more grateful we become. And after a while it becomes a habit that has the power to make us more optimistic, which, as we know, increases our overall senses of joy, hope, and vitality.

There is a tendency for most people to live in a state of want and longing, as if there is something *out there* that we need in order to be happy. This state of mind produces certain results in our lives, and those results usually include anxiety, over-working, disappointment, anger, and ultimately despair, as long as we continue to dwell on what we *don't* have.

It's tempting to simply wait for something appreciation-worthy to emerge before being grateful. This is the mark of pessimistic thinking because of which our expectations are at such a high level that things we would normally appreciate are seen as the status quo or bare minimum, and thus unworthy of gratitude. But once we begin looking for things to appreciate in others, the material to work with is nearly endless. It's all there, and it just takes some slowing down to recognize it.

The more we do this, the better we get at it. Admittedly, it can be uncomfortable at first if it's not a regular habit. Making a point to stop and tell someone we appreciate something about him or her may at first be outside our comfort zones or what we believe is characteristic of our personalities. But being out of practice doesn't mean it's not possible to become good at something. It simply means we haven't been in the habit of practicing it.

But as we practice it, it becomes easier and less awkward to stop and say to a roommate or spouse, "I noticed you did all the dishes in the sink, both yours and mine. Thanks so much for doing that," or to a friend, "Last time I saw you, when I was having a tough time, you were so patient and listened to me. Thank you so much. It meant a lot."

As we make this a habit, we begin to see life differently—as abundant and loving. We begin to feel a sense of contentment with our jobs and our communities and see the world as full of promise and opportunity. Our ways of *being* change, which begins to open up new possibilities. This becomes a cycle of goodness in our lives. As more opportunities arise from this state of being, we have even more to appreciate, and thus achieve better results in life.

Are you willing to take a minute right now and begin your "I'm Thankful For" list? Think about what you're thankful for in regards to your job, community, group of friends, living situation, opportunities to serve, singing voice, business talents, significant other, and any other area of your life.

Epilogue

It's time. The day has come to pursue your dreams with the sense that everything is possible and available to you, no matter what anyone else thinks or believes.

And, trust me, I know this is no easy thing. You've got your own intrinsic limiting voices and maybe even the audible voices of the people around you. The voices are repeating common rackets, like, "You're not good enough," or, "You'll be judged," or, "It's too risky."

But here's the thing: playing small does not serve the world. In fact, it harms the world and robs them of your gifts and contributions.

It's time. Today is the day.

Okay, understood? Great.

So, here's the thing: if you really want to transform your life, follow the principles laid out in this book. Don't just half-ass it. Remember, information alone isn't transformational. It's the application of that information that produces results.

Even if you just take one of the principles in this book and commit to applying it to your life over the course of the next 2-3 weeks, that alone will begin the seed of transformation that can multiply radically over time and shift the results you're getting in your life. Don't set this book down without choosing one or two principles to begin applying today. You can come back in a few weeks and apply one or two more.

Applying these principles in sequences is important because the human mind can't process clusters of ideas without feeling overwhelmed, stressed, and prematurely defeated. So if that's how you're feeling after having finished this book, it may be because you are trying to juggle too many new ideas at once, which may prevent you from being able to implement even one of them successfully.

Remember, stress always follows the unmanageable lists of things we need to do. Instead of allowing fear to paralyze you, apply the principles in sequences or bite-sized bits so you can start today.

Here are the principles of the book pared down for you to help you begin this process.

Ready?

1. Can I Become a Great _____?

Greatness starts through transformation of your *way of being*. The powers of choice and self-determination are not outside of you but within you. Give yourself permission to use them.

2. I Just Don't Know *How*

Believing we don't know how to do something is a cover we use to hide the fact that we are not yet determined enough to reach our goals. Once we crank up our desire to achieve to a critical mass, "how to" becomes obvious.

3. I Need More Information First

We may hide behind not having enough information to avoid getting started, thinking we are being prudent by avoiding risk. Fear of failure, hidden under the guise of seeking information, can keep us stuck in life.

4. Who Am I?

Understanding your personality is interesting but becomes confining when we think of it as a fixed, unchanging attribute. We choose who we want to be—our personalities are our own creations.

5. Mind-Shift

Our perceptions of the world are informed by the language we use to describe it, and our behavior stems from the way we see the world. This means that we can improve our behavior by using more generative and resourceful language.

6. Everything's Going To S#*!
The way we define our realities sets the framework for how our lives and circumstances will unfold—so we can choose to ground our actions in a framework of possibility rather than in the stuck place of downward spiral thinking.

7. My Life Isn't Working
Usually it's not a circumstance or a person holding us back from realizing our potential; it's the victim narrative we use to describe the world. Seeing ourselves as victims deprives us of agency and kills our mood, motivation, and energy.

8. I Can't Get Beyond This Ceiling
We have an inner thermostat, programmed in childhood, that determines how much love, success, creativity, and wealth we will allow ourselves to have. But it can be reprogrammed to accommodate greater prosperity.

9. I'm Frustrated
Frustration is a resistance to reality and an alternative to creating something new. It's a way of dwelling on past hurts rather than formulating a new vision.

10. Fantasy

Often our perceptions contradict reality. When there's a gap between our perception and reality, it's difficult to gain traction toward our goals.

11. Reality

When living in fantasy there's a gap between our intentions and our impacts on the world. The quickest way to close that gap and realign with reality is to seek feedback.

12. Am I In Breakdown?

We can pull ourselves out of the stuck place of breakdown by identifying it, owning it, forgiving ourselves, and making a new commitment toward a clear vision.

13. Sorry I'm Late

The impact of a broken commitment not only impacts another person's trust in us; it also decreases our own confidence in ourselves and our abilities to create change.

14. Seriously?

Obsessing over looking good, feeling good, being right, and being in control are common ways we take ourselves too seriously. These preoccupations prevent us from seeking feedback or gaining traction toward our desired results.

15. Tell Someone

We do better when others are watching. The principle of external accountability uses the ego against itself to produce the results that we really want in life.

16. Requests

There are two main ways to shape your future: promises and requests. Ambitious people ask for what they want. Don't say "no" for anyone else. The world is ready to say "yes."

17. Freedom Addict

Discipline equals freedom. Freedom in our lives comes not from seeking to do whatever we want but instead implementing discipline and routine in our lives.

18. The Momentum Fulcrum

Momentum helps us go further and faster more effortlessly. It is a powerful force; but only after we do the tough initial work of committing and getting into action.

19. The Habit

All habits are malleable. We have the power to form and reform any habit. We do so first by believing it's possible and then by understanding both the habit loop and the power of rewards.

20. The Un-Had Conversation

The un-had conversation is the one dictating your live. The things we avoid hold the reins in our lives, and often the solution is simply initiating a difficult conversation.

21. He Doesn't Deserve It

Holding grudges surrenders power and agency to the people or circumstances we choose not to forgive. Forgiveness frees us from that tyranny and restores the agency of the offended and offending party.

22. I Apologize

An "apology" is a defense of, or a justification for, something we've done; while seeking forgiveness honors the offended party and fully restores trust in the relationship.

23. Thanks, Man

Our way of *being* changes when we choose to practice the discipline of gratitude, as does our sense of peace and well-being. Create an "I'm Thankful For" list and review it often. Through gratitude, we see the world as more resourceful and gain traction toward our dreams.

Would You Do Me a Favor?

If you enjoyed *Your Prosperous Mind,* would you mind taking a minute and writing a review on Amazon? Even a short review helps, and it'd mean a lot to me.

If someone you care about is stuck in life or you think they would benefit from the principles in this book, please send them a copy. I would really appreciate it whether you gift it to them on Amazon or email them a copy of the PDF.

If you'd like to order copies of this book for your company, organization, or group of friends, please go to www. yourprosperousmind.com for more information.

Finally, if you'd like to get free bonus materials from this book and receive updates on my future projects you can sign up for my email list at www.yourprosperousmind. com. You can also follow me on Twitter and Instagram@ AaronAnastasi.

Acknowledgments

First of all, I would like to thank my wife, Martha. Not only is she the greatest thing that's ever happened to me, aside from maybe my faith in God, but she is the most supportive lifemate anyone could ask for. She constantly supports and encourages me to chase after my dreams—this book being one of them.

Also, a portion of the chapters in this book were originally in my first book, *The Voice of Your Dreams*, but because of the extreme length of that book's initial draft, I cut a fair amount of the content and placed some of it here in this book. This means that those who helped out with the first book are credited, at least in part, for the completion and quality of this book as well.

Among them are my beta readers who helped me significantly raise the level and quality of this book's content and flow: Autumn "Fladmo" Smith, Hank Fortener, Jeff Holder, Jordan Shappell, Anthony Chiles, Matt Dalton, Britney Dalton, Tana Anastasia, Jordan Owen, Shannon

M. Taylor, Kelly Johnson, and Christie McGuire. Thank you all for your honesty and your time. I'm indebted to you.

Chas Smith and Matt Smith—ideal business partners and long-time, loyal friend—are the ones who journeyed with me as co-founders of Superior Singing Method. They also helped fund the completion and launch of this book.

To Dane Sanders who helped me overcome many obstacles in creating this book.

To my feedback crew who endured endless emails about cover content and design: Jordan Owen, Morgan Owen, David Magidoff, Sarah Magidoff, Angela Mukul, Joby Harris, Shannon M. Taylor, Meg Miller, and Johnny Young.

To those who influenced me along the way: Werner Erhard, Byron Katie, Dan Tocchini, Martha Beck, Steve Chandler, Rich Litvin, Steven Pressfield, Erwin McManus, and Tim Ferriss. And, of course, to Andy Stanley, a mentor and friend whose teachings and life shaped my young adulthood.

To my brilliant editor Chelsea Richardson.

To my book endorsers: Robert Allan Ackerman, Cress Williams, Matt Mugford, and Nathan Chapman.

About the Author

Aaron Anastasi was born in Orange County, California — surfing, playing guitar, and performing musical theater. With a love for adventure, Anastasi was a pro snowboarder in Vail, Colorado, scaled Glacier Lake mountains in Bolivia, and cut pathways through the jungles of Contagem, Brazil. While pursing his degrees in Humanities at Lee University  (B.A.) and Princeton (M.Div.), he spent summers and weekends touring widely and performing music, sketches, and stand up comedy. Now he resides in Los Angeles, California where he works as a writer, actor, life coach, and producer. He also hosts the globally recognized "Superior Singing Method," an online singing lesson program that he created. His other online businesses include "Superior Songwriting Method," "Play Worship Guitar," and "Signing Success."

60762398R00124

Made in the USA
San Bernardino, CA
13 December 2017